THE ENGLISH CHURCH IN THE EIGHTEENTH CENTURY

OTHER BOOKS BY DR. SYDNEY CARTER

THE ENGLISH CHURCH AND THE REFORMATION
THE ENGLISH CHURCH IN THE 17TH CENTURY
THE ENGLISH CHURCH IN THE 18TH CENTURY
MINISTERIAL COMMISSION
THE REFORMATION AND REUNION
ETC., ETC.

THE ENGLISH CHURCH IN THE EIGHTEENTH CENTURY

By

C. SYDNEY CARTER,

M.A., D.D., F.R.Hist.S.

PRINCIPAL OF CLIFTON THEOLOGICAL COLLEGE 1932–46

LONDON

CHURCH BOOK ROOM PRESS LTD.

7, WINE OFFICE COURT, FLEET STREET, E.C.4

1948

First published . . . 1910
Second Edition . . . 1948

PREFACE TO SECOND EDITION

THE second edition of this short history will enable Churchmen and others to read in a compact and handy form a short concise account of the religious and social conditions prevailing in England in the eighteenth century. To an alarming extent, then as now, Christianity was attacked, ridiculed, scorned, or merely ignored, as an outworn or dangerous superstition, which had for too long interrupted the freedom and pleasures of mankind. It is therefore both heartening and inspiring to read of the marvellous spiritual awakening produced by the great Methodist and Evangelical revival in that century. It gives us hope and confidence as we pray for a similar divine intervention and outpouring of God's grace in our own times, when "the darkness shall turn to the dawning" which shall usher in another revival of true religion and piety which may then "be established among us."

C. S. C.

BRISTOL,
Sept. 1947.

PREFACE

THIS little book is intended as a companion volume to one recently published in the same series, entitled *The English Church in the Seventeenth Century*, and its aim is similar.

The eighteenth century is too often regarded as a somewhat gloomy, uninteresting, and uninspiring period of Church history, and as a consequence its study has been largely neglected. It is therefore hoped that an attempt to give a concise and popular outline of the life and work of the Church during this century, so conspicuous for its religious and moral degeneration, may prove both interesting and instructive, and once more furnish an illustration of the truth that the darkest hours in the life of the Christian Church have usually been but the prelude to a bright dawn of revived spiritual life and vigour.

Amongst other valuable Church historians of the period, I would desire to acknowledge a special indebtedness to Messrs. Abbey and Overton's thorough and comprehensive work *The English Church in the Eighteenth Century*.

HERNE BAY,
June 1910.

PRINCIPAL EVENTS

1698. Formation of the Society for Promoting Christian Knowledge.
1701. Formation of the Society for the Propagation of the Gospel.
1709. Trial of Dr. Sacheverell.
1711. Occasional Conformity Act passed.
1714. {Schism Act passed.
Death of Queen Anne.
1717. The Bangorian Controversy leads to the silencing of Convocation.
1718. Archbishop Wake corresponds with the Gallican Church.
1723. Trial and banishment of Bishop Atterbury.
1729. Oxford Methodists formed.
1730. Publication of *Christianity as Old as the Creation.*
1735. John and Charles Wesley visit Georgia.
1736. Publication of Bishop Butler's *Analogy*.
1737. John Potter succeeds to the Primacy.
1738. {John Wesley returns from Georgia.
Whitefield goes to Georgia.
1739. Wesley commences field preaching.
1740. Establishment of the Methodist Society.
1741. Wesley employs lay preachers.
1744. First Wesleyan Conference.
1747. Thomas Herring becomes Archbishop of Canterbury.
1750. David Hume's *Essays* published.
1758. Thomas Secker appointed to the Primacy.
1760. Methodists begin to license their chapels.
1766. Blackburne's *Confessional* published.
1768. Cornwallis succeeds to the Primacy.
1770. Death of George Whitefield.
1771. Feathers Tavern Petition against Subscription.
1776. Gibbon's *Decline and Fall of the Roman Empire* published.
1781. {Lady Huntingdon registers her chapels.
Raikes commences the Sunday-school movement.

1784. Wesley ordains Dr. Coke.
Consecration of Samuel Seabury.

1787. William Wilberforce starts Anti-Slave Trade Crusade.
Consecration of Dr. Charles Inglis as first Bishop of the Colonial Church.

1791. Death of John Wesley.

1794. Paine's *Age of Reason* published.

1795. London Missionary Society founded.
Wesleyan Conference sanctions administration of the Sacrament in Methodist chapels.

1799. Formation of Church Missionary Society.
Formation of Religious Tract Society.

1804. Formation of the British and Foreign Bible Society.

CONTENTS

CHAPTER I

INTRODUCTION

THE eighteenth century may be considered as severing the last link between mediæval and modern Church history. The religious strife of the sixteenth century had culminated in the revolt of many of the various national churches against the old idea of universal Christendom under one absolute ruler. The Reformation had successfully vindicated the principle of nationality in religion and the right of individual churches to regulate their own doctrine and discipline in accordance with their conception of primitive and Catholic usage. The English and Continental Reformers had been practically united in their struggle to free themselves from the corruptions of mediæval Christianity by an appeal to the supreme authority of Holy Scripture and the right of private judgment in matters of faith. In England they had been completely victorious, and the seventeenth century saw a strong national Church restored to primitive catholicity and freed from Papal domination. Scarcely, however, had this great victory been achieved when contention broke out *within* its borders concerning the precise character of the government and discipline of the Reformed Church. This religious controversy became associated with a great political struggle, with the unfortunate result that the Protestant cause in England was seriously weakened by a permanent division in its ranks. The failure to effect a compromise between these contending parties in 1662, largely owing to the dominant spirit of revenge and suspicion, had resulted in the expulsion of the Presbyterians from the national Church and the foundation of permanently organised nonconformity in England.

A lamentable and futile attempt to exact a universal conformity to the established religion, by a harsh system of persecution and proscription, had at last ended at the Revolution by the frank recognition of the principle of toleration, and Churchmen soon learnt to their surprise that the penal laws had been more conducive to the progress of Dissent than the dreaded **Toleration Act** of 1689.

The controversies, however, which disturbed the Church in the eighteenth century were of an entirely different character.

It was now no longer a question of "Protestant" or "Papist," the exterior of the building had been definitely defined; the strife, also, was ended as to whether there was room in the interior for Arminians and Calvinists or for Episcopalians and Presbyterians. The struggle was now of a far more serious character and centred round the very foundations of the building itself.

Doctrinal disputes had given place to philosophical, infidel, and sceptical attacks on the fundamental doctrines of the Christian faith. The reaction from the stern discipline and severe morality of the Puritans had resulted in a deplorable spread of licentiousness, immorality, and indifference. A spirit of precise theological dogmatism was succeeded by one of vague philosophical speculation. Thus the old religious controversies almost entirely ceased and fresh ones raged round the nature of God and the Person of Christ; and the Church had to repel the attacks of Deists on the one hand and Arians and Socinians on the other. The revival of the spirit of Philosophical investigation led also to a revival of the disputes and speculations which rent the Early Church concerning the divinity of Christ.

The Church soon felt the influence of this change, and the close of the seventeenth century had witnessed the rise of an influential body of intellectual Churchmen who, by their broad and somewhat indefinite theological views, soon earned for themselves the name of "Latitudinarian." They showed a dangerous tendency to undervalue the importance of divine revelation and to subordinate every question to the supreme test of reason. Christianity was appealed to as much because it was a reasonable system inculcating virtue, culture, and refinement, as because its inherent truth and vitality proved its divine origin. By the beginning of the next century this new school of divines had become very powerful, and grew in influence and importance as it advanced. The closing years of the seventeenth century had also seen a temporary revival of religious zeal and enterprise in the commencement of missionary effort and in the formation of religious societies to restrain the vice and profanity of the times; but these earnest efforts were of short duration, and before the beginning of the next generation we enter a period of religious decadence and stagnation which has caused the eighteenth century to be regarded as one of the darkest in the annals of English Church history. On the accession of Anne in 1702, however, the Church was on the floodtide of popularity and enthusiasm, and there seemed little outward evidence of the fearful decay of real Christianity which so soon followed.

CHAPTER II

ANNE AND HIGH CHURCH POPULARITY

THE new Sovereign was in her religious convictions a marked contrast to her predecessor. William III. had been educated as a Presbyterian, and although during his reign in England he had conformed to the established religion, he had never any peculiar attachment for or sympathy with its special form of government and worship. Widely tolerant by nature and liberal in his religious views, he had chosen men who sympathised with his own religious and political opinions as the leaders of the Church, and thus the bishops appointed during his reign, although conspicuous for their piety, learning, and ability, were almost entirely of Whig and moderate Latitudinarian sympathies. Anne, on the other hand had been brought up as a strict Churchwoman and was zealously attached to the Anglican communion, and thus her accession was hailed with enthusiasm by the Tories and High Churchmen with whose views she was known to sympathise. One of the first evidences of this change was seen in the dissolution of a commission of bishops which William had appointed to advise him concerning Church patronage. This commission had excited the greatest animosity of the High Churchmen from the political and party character of its ecclesiastical appointments. Anne also told her first Parliament that " I shall always make it my own particular care to encourage and maintain the Church as by law established, and every the least member of it in all their just rights and privileges, and upon all occasions of promotion to any ecclesiastical dignity I shall have a very just regard to such as are eminent and remarkable for their piety, learning, and constant zeal for the Church." [1]

In 1704 the Queen gave a very practical token of this affection and regard for the Church by voluntarily resigning her right to the first-fruits and tenths of benefices, which previous to an

[1] Tindal's Continuation of Rapin's *Hist. of Eng.*, vol. iv. Bk. xxvi. p. 372.

Act passed by Henry VIII. had been paid to the Popes but since that time had been appropriated by the Crown. Anne now desired Parliament to pass an Act applying these funds for the augmentation of poor livings, and under the name of "Queen Anne's Bounty" this generous benefaction has been an incalculable boon to the Church.

One of the prominent features of the ecclesiastical history of Anne's reign was the incessant disputes in Convocation between the High and Broad or Latitudinarian Church parties. These quarrels had arisen at the close of the last reign owing to a claim advanced by the lower House, which was mainly composed of High Churchmen, to debate, adjourn, or prorogue independently of the action of the Bishops in the Upper House. This claim, which was contrary to precedent, had been stoutly resisted by the Primate and the Whig Bishops, who could ill brook the obstinate, intemperate, and undignified opposition of the inferior clergy under the able leadership of Atterbury, an acute controversialist. The death of William III. had produced a temporary lull in the storm, but the bitter quarrels were at once resumed at the first session of Convocation in the new reign.

The right of separate prorogation was again asserted by the Lower House but rejected by the Upper, although Archbishop Tenison offered the presbyters the privilege of meeting in committees between the sessions. Not content with this, the Lower House desired that the question might be submitted to the decision of the Queen. The Bishops rejected this proposal on the ground that it displayed a want of deference to the spiritual fathers of the Church. This aspersion the presbyters indignantly repudiated, declaring that they regarded the order of Bishops "to be of divine apostolic institution," and they requested the Upper House to concur in this resolution. As the majority of the Bishops certainly did not believe in the divine apostolic institution of episcopacy, this challenge placed them in an awkward position. The Archbishop, however, evaded the question by informing the Lower House that such a declaration was equivalent to making a canon, for which they had no royal license.

In 1704 the Lower House made a formal "Representation" to the Bishops complaining of a want of Church discipline and several irregularities and abuses which reflected on the negligence of the Bishops, "but took no care to insist upon those greater abuses of pluralities, non-residence, neglect of cures, and the irregularities of the lives of the clergy which were too visible." [1] The Archbishop made a temperate and conciliatory reply to this complaint, vindicating the care and diligence of the bishops in their frequent visitations, and their zeal in missionary effort and in the promotion of charity schools and the instruction of the young. [2]

The disputes continued with unceasing bitterness during the following year, the Primate severely censuring the Lower House for holding a session independently of the Upper. In 1706 the Lower House refused to concur in the address to the Crown voted by the Bishops, and claimed the right of presenting a separate one of their own. At this juncture the Archbishop obtained the intervention of the Queen, who wrote a letter severely censuring these unseemly disputes and declaring her resolve "to maintain her supremacy over the Church and the due subordination of presbyters to Bishops as fundamental parts thereof." Convocation was then prorogued, and at the next session was not allowed to transact any business. The Lower House protested vigorously against these immediate prorogations as unprecedented, but this action brought upon them a severe reprimand from the Queen, who declared that the protest "was an invasion of her royal supremacy, reposed in her by the law and constitution of the Church of England, and that if anything of like nature was attempted for the future it would make it necessary for her to use such means for punishing offences of this nature as are warranted by law." [3]

This was a signal triumph for the Upper House, but when Convocation next met in 1711 the political horizon had entirely changed. The trial of Sacheverell had resulted in a strong Tory reaction, and the Whigs were driven from office; thus there was little fear of any hindrance being placed in the way of the action of the Church "Parliament." The Queen, under the guidance of Archbishop Sharp, her chief spiritual adviser, issued a licence to Convocation to debate on several pressing subjects, including the growth of heresy and infidelity, the regulation of proceedings in excommunication, the preparation of forms for visiting prisoners and the admission of converts from the Romish Church, and the regulation of licences for matrimony to prevent more effectually clandestine marriages.

Unfortunately the good results which might have followed

[1] Tindal's Continuation of Rapin, vol. iv. Bk. xxvi. pp. 374 and 408.
[2] Ibid., p. 409. [3] Ibid., p. 500.

from the consideration of these practical questions were prevented by a prosecution for heresy, which occupied the remaining time of both Houses. A book written by William Whiston, a Cambridge professor, entitled *Historical Preface to Primitive Christianity Revived*, was condemned by both Houses as "directly opposite to the fundamental articles of the Christian religion." The important question then arose as to the right of Convocation to judge matters of heresy, but the judges eventually decided this in the affirmative, and the censure was sent to the Queen, who, however, allowed the whole matter to drop. The next session was wholly occupied with disputes between the two Houses as to the order of procedure, and no business whatever was transacted, but in 1714 Convocation again received "Letters of Business" authorising it to treat on the subjects previously brought before it; but again its labours were interrupted by the consideration of the opinions of Dr. Samuel Clarke on the subject of the Holy Trinity. In attempting to give a reasonable explanation of this deep and mysterious doctrine, Clarke had departed unintentionally from the orthodox faith. Before any definite action had been taken, however, the death of the Queen put an end to the proceedings. Thus the special opportunity for useful and practical Church legislation which this reign seemed destined to afford was almost entirely lost, owing to the unprofitable discussions as to rights and precedents, largely engendered by the unfortunate political and party character of the two Houses.

Although the High Church party had been unsuccessful in their struggle with the Upper House of Convocation, their power and influence throughout this reign were exceedingly great; in fact, the popularity of the Church, and particularly the High Church section, was a prominent characteristic of the period. The Lower House of Convocation had a large body of supporters in the House of Commons even during the ascendency of the Whigs, while the Tories were High Churchmen almost to a man. In 1702 the Commons passed a resolution that they would "on all occasions assert the just rights and privileges of the Lower House of Convocation," [1] and again in 1710 they promised to receive its recommendations "with particular regard."

The first evidence of this strength of the Church party in Parliament was the attempt made to pass what afterwards was known as the "Occasional Conformity Bill." It had been the practice of a large number of Nonconformists to evade the severe

[1] Tindal's *Rapin*, vol. iv. p. 374.

restrictions of the Test Act by occasionally receiving the Sacrament of the Lord's Supper in church as a qualification for office. This prostitution of a most sacred religious rite was especially reprehensible to High Churchmen, and they were determined to exert every effort to prevent it. Unfortunately, however, mixed up with this laudable desire there was an ulterior aim in the minds of many to deprive the Dissenters once more of the religious liberty they enjoyed under the Toleration Act. Thus in 1702 a Bill was introduced compelling Nonconformists to serve the offices for which a sacramental test was necessary, but refusing to accept a single reception as a sufficient compliance with the terms of the Test Act. Heavy fines were inflicted on all officials attending a conventicle. The Act did not attempt to forbid Dissenters receiving the sacrament in their parish churches, but imposed a heavy fine on the Dissenter if during the next twelve months he attended a Conventicle. The confirmation rubric was never appealed to in order to prevent this occasional Conformity.[1] Burnet says that "the sharpness with which (the supporters of this measure) treated the Dissenters in all their speeches showed as if they designed their extirpation."[2] This Bill soon received the support of the Commons, but as the Lords considered some of its provisions too severe it was dropped, owing to a want of agreement between the two Houses.

The Bill was again brought forward in 1703 and passed the Commons by a large majority, but it was strongly opposed by Bishop Burnet in the Lords, who argued that a revival of persecution would weaken rather than safeguard the Church. The majority of the Bishops voted against the measure and the Lords rejected it. The next year it met with the same fate, although it was well known that the Queen desired its enactment. The Whigs having obtained a majority in the Commons in 1705, the Occasional Conformity Bill was for a time dropped, but a furious agitation in its favour was kept up by the Tories in the country. A pamphlet written by Dr. Drake entitled *A Memorial of the Church of England*, made a violent attack on the Government for betraying the interests of the Church, and created such a panic amongst Churchmen that a debate was held in Parliament on the subject. In the House of Lords the motion that the "Church was in danger" was opposed by the Whig Bishops and rejected by 61 to 30. The Commons also arrived at the same

[1] A sufficient proof that its provisions applied only to Churchmen.
[2] *His Own Times*, iii. p. 467 (1753).

decision, and a royal proclamation was issued stating that the Church of England was in "a most safe and flourishing condition."[1]

But this intolerant and fanatical spirit displayed in the Commons by High Church Tories was by no means the only evidence of the strength and popularity of the High Church party. It was still more conspicuously demonstrated by an incident which occurred in 1709. The appointment of two High Churchmen to the Episcopal Bench had revived the old controversies concerning the divine right of kings and the doctrine of passive obedience. Tory Churchmen were everywhere proclaiming that the "Church was in danger," and denouncing in the most violent language the policy of the Whig Government as tending to subvert the national religion. One of the most hot-headed of these semi-political and semi-ecclesiastical enthusiasts was Dr. Henry Sacheverell, a bombastic preacher of mediocre ability, who, owing to the very injudicious action of the Whig ministry, acquired fame and popularity far surpassing his merits. Sacheverell had preached a powerful but truculent sermon before the Lord Mayor, containing scandalous accusations and reflections on the Government. From the text "In perils among false brethren" he charged the Whigs with a sinful betrayal of the Church by secret treachery; they were the false brethren "who let her worst adversaries into her bowels under the holy umbrage of sons, who neither believe her faith, own her mission, submit to her discipline, nor comply with her liturgy."

Unfortunately this passionate effusion, instead of being treated with the contempt it deserved, was brought to the notice of the Commons, and it was decided to impeach Sacheverell before the House of Lords, "for defaming the Revolution, condemning toleration, asserting the Church to be in danger, and proclaiming her Majesty's advisers to be false brethren and traitors to the Church and State." Immediately Sacheverell became a popular hero. Multitudes followed his coach with cheers as he drove to his trial; the mob rallied to the cry of "Sacheverell and High Church." Meeting-houses were burnt or pulled down, and the soldiers were required to quell the disturbances. Even the Queen's coach was surrounded by crowds shouting "God bless your Majesty; we hope your Majesty is for High Church and Dr. Sacheverell." The trial lasted about a month, and in the end Sacheverell was declared guilty by the Lords by 69 to 52;

[1] Tindal's *Rapin*, vol. iv. p. 460.

but so strong and menacing was the popular feeling on his behalf, in which the Queen was suspected to share, that the Commons contented themselves with passing a ridiculous sentence suspending him for three years from preaching and ordering his sermon to be burnt by the common hangman.[1] This punishment was hailed with unbounded rejoicing throughout the country, and Sacheverell was everywhere loaded with honours and congratulations, the Queen bestowing a rich living upon him. Parliament was dissolved, and the new House of Commons contained an overwhelming number of Tories and High Churchmen, who governed the country till the close of the reign.

This change of ministry enabled the High Church party to carry their **Occasional Conformity Bill,** which was passed without a division in both Houses in 1711. In 1714 the spirit of religious persecution was carried still farther by the passing of the **Schism Act,** which forbade, under penalty of imprisonment without bail, any person to keep a public or private school unless he conformed to the English Church and had obtained a licence from the Bishop. It was contended that the Dissenters were inveterate enemies of the Church, and therefore their schools were a great danger to its safety. Fortunately the provisions of this arbitrary measure were never enforced, and both this and the Occasional Conformity Act were repealed in 1718.

Happily the great popularity and influence of the Church at this time were not in any way dependent on these repressive measures, but were due rather to its increasing religious and literary zeal. Although it was a period when the social position and public esteem of the clergy, as a body, seem to have been very low, yet it was none the less conspicuous for the brilliant intellectual attainments of many of the most eminent divines. It was, however, unfortunate that their literary talents and abilities should have been directed so largely into a political rather than a distinctly religious channel, but this was mainly due to the heated party spirit of the times. Probably the most able of these political ecclesiastics was Jonathan Swift, Dean of St. Patrick's, whose clever satires rendered great service to the Tory party. The Whigs, however, found equal support from the powerful sermons and writings of the celebrated Benjamin Hoadly against the doctrine of "passive obedience." But theological treatises of the very first order were by no means neglected when we recall the writings of Bishop Bull in the

[1] *Cf.* Tindal's *Rapin,* vol. iv. pp. 588–95.

Defence of the Nicene Faith and his *Judicium Ecclesiæ Catholicæ*, or William Wall's exhaustive treatise on the *History of Infant Baptism*, while the valuable works of Dean Prideaux in his *Connection of Sacred and Profane History* and Joseph Bingham's *Origines Ecclesiasticæ* must by no means be overlooked.

But the Church of Anne's reign was as equally renowned for its religious zeal as for its literary activity. At the close of the last reign the two now famous societies, one for the dissemination of religious literature, the **Society for Promoting Christian Knowledge,** the other for the encouragement of foreign missionary effort, the **Society for the Propagation of the Gospel,** had been founded and were carrying on their work with energy and self-sacrifice. Religious and devotional societies of young men, and societies for the suppression of vice and the reformation of manners, had also been established in William's reign, and these were now spreading in most of the larger towns and doing very valuable work. The character of sermons had greatly improved, and daily and weekly services became far more frequent. "Within the cities of London and Westminster," we are told, "in most churches there be constant prayers morning and evening." [1] The Holy Communion was celebrated much more frequently, many parish churches, as well as all cathedrals, having weekly administrations. "On every Lord's Day, in London, there were constant sacraments in many churches, greater numbers attended, and greater appearances of devotion were diffused through the city than had been observed in the memory of man." [2] Money had been voted for the erection of fifty new churches in London, although, owing to the death of the Queen, only twelve were actually built. Parochial libraries for the supply of religious and moral literature, sorely needed to counteract the deplorable tone of popular writings, were started in many places, while as many as fifty-four Charity Schools were at work in London alone. With all these earnest efforts and practical Christian work the Queen was known to be in the fullest sympathy, and thus, especially in view of the careless and indifferent character of her successor, her death was regarded as a severe blow to the good work which the Church was accomplishing. In spite of this drawback, and also of the baneful influence of Walpole's administration, it is still very remarkable that such great religious zeal and activity should so quickly have been

[1] Paterson, *Pietas Londinensis*, 1714, Intro.
[2] Quoted in Hutton, *Hist. of Eng. Ch. 1660–1714*, p. 305.

superseded by the cold and colourless Christianity which soon became a marked feature of the Hanoverian period.

CHAPTER III

THE GROWTH OF LATITUDINARIANISM

THE accession of George I. introduces us to an entirely new era in English Church history. The change of dynasty had an immediate effect on the position of Church parties; the High Churchmen almost at once lost their influence and ascendency and sank into insignificance. Tenaciously adhering to their doctrine of "divine right," they looked with no favour on a foreign king with a merely parliamentary title to the Crown, and one who, unlike his predecessor, had no peculiar affection for or interest in the Church of which he was the temporal head. Thus those of them who gave a reluctant allegiance to the new government were regarded with suspicion as at best secret Jacobites and unfit for promotion to influential positions. The rebellion of 1715 was a forcible illustration that the Hanoverian dynasty was by no means secured from Jacobite intrigues, and therefore it was all-important to enlist on its side the powerful support of a great national institution like the Church. Unfortunately, however, these peculiar political conditions had a disastrous effect on its life and influence.

Sir Robert Walpole, the minister whose power was paramount throughout this reign, in his endeavour to preserve the Protestant succession adopted the prudent policy of silencing all antagonistic influences and allaying all religious controversies likely to disturb the peace of the kingdom. With this end in view, ecclesiastical preferments were lavished entirely on those Churchmen who could be relied on for steadily supporting the reigning dynasty, and as these were confined mainly to men of Whig politics and Latitudinarian principles, this type of churchmanship soon became predominant. High Churchmen were silenced, party strife almost entirely ceased, and under the guidance of Whig Bishops the Church soon degenerated into a mere national establishment to be used as a powerful instrument for safeguarding the interests of the reigning political party.

One event which occurred soon after the accession of the new

Sovereign probably did more than anything else to stifle the life and energies of the Church during the rest of the century. In 1717 the famous "Bangorian Controversy" directly led to the silencing of Convocation for over a century. Benjamin Hoadly, who was responsible for this calamity, was the Whig Bishop of Bangor and an ardent controversialist, advocating strong Latitudinarian views, peculiarly reprehensible to his High Church contemporaries. In 1716 he wrote a reply to a book published by a Non-juring Bishop (George Hickes), which had accused all who held communion with the national Church as wicked and wilful schismatics. This bold denunciation was ably refuted by Hoadly, who, to expose fully the arrogant pretensions of his opponent, advanced the highly contentious theory that the only *necessary* test of a true Christian profession is *sincerity*, and not communion with any visible church. In 1717 he preached a sermon before the King on the "Nature of the Kingdom or Church of Christ," in which he scoffed at the importance of tests of orthodoxy, maintaining that the Church was identical with the Kingdom of Heaven, and that Christ left behind no visible human authority, no vicegerents; no judges over the consciences or religion of his people."[1]

These novel views were assailed on all sides, and Hoadly was virulently attacked for the supposed tendency of his statements. The Lower House reported that his doctrines tended to subvert all government and discipline in the Church of Christ, as well as to impeach the royal supremacy in ecclesiastical cases. The Government, however, which regarded Hoadly as the champion of the Whig cause, ordered the immediate prorogation of Convocation in order to avert an express condemnation of his writings or sermon by the two Houses. Convocation was not allowed to meet again for regular business till 1852. The controversy was, however, continued through the medium of the press, and four of Hoadly's principal opponents were deprived of their positions as Royal Chaplains on account of their strenuous opposition to the Court favourite. Probably the most able refutation of Hoadly's opinions came from the pen of William Law, a young man, then scarcely known, whose masterly defence[2] of Church principles established his reputation as a controversialist of no mean order.

In 1722 occurred the important trial of Francis Atterbury,

[1] Quoted in Overton and Relton, *Hist. of Eng. Ch. 1714–1800*, p. 16.
[2] Entitled *Three Letters to the Bishop of Bangor*.

Bishop of Rochester. A brilliant preacher and a famous Tory orator, he had first won fame in William III.'s reign by his able and trenchant advocacy of the rights of the Lower House of Convocation. He was now the recognised leader of the High Church clergy, an ardent Jacobite, and most strenuous in his opposition to the new Government. It was reported that on the death of Anne he had offered publicly to proclaim "James III." as her successor, and since then he had been in constant intercourse with the exiled Stuarts, and in 1722 was implicated in a conspiracy to restore the Pretender. It is difficult to determine the exact extent of his complicity, but he was arrested and confined to the Tower, where he appears to have received very harsh treatment. The Commons proceeded against him by the arbitrary method of a Bill of Pains and Penalties, which was easily carried. Atterbury made a very able defence when the case came before the Lords, but the Bill was passed, and he was deprived of his See and banished for life. He withdrew to France and continued his active support of the Stuart cause. But although condemned by Parliament, his popularity amongst the clergy and people was very great. Deep sympathy was shown towards him while in prison, and "under pretence of his being afflicted with gout, he was publicly prayed for in most of the churches of London and Westminster, and there was spread among the people a pathetic print of the bishop looking through the bars of his prison and holding in his hand a portrait of Archbishop Laud."[1] His fall and banishment were a great blow to the High Church and Jacobite clergy, as it brought their ecclesiastical as well as their political opinions into disrepute and still further encouraged the promotion of clergy of Latitudinarian views, who now became virtually supreme in the Church.

It is well here to consider more particularly the theological views and tendencies of this powerful school of divines, and notice the change and development of their teaching since their rise towards the close of the previous century. The movement originally had been largely a reaction against the narrow and dogmatic theology of the Puritans on the one hand and the rigid and exclusive Church views of extreme Arminians on the other, and at first had little or no tendency towards unorthodoxy. Thus in their practical aims they had striven earnestly to reunite Churchmen and Dissenters, and although their methods for this general "comprehension" of all Christians may have been open to

[1] Quoted in Lord Mahon's *Hist. of Eng.*, ii. 38 (1853).

question, and certainly were little in harmony with the narrow ecclesiasticism of the age, yet their central plea for a liberal and comprehensive spirit in religious matters, despite the excesses to which it too often led, was thoroughly vindicated by their more speculative successors in the eighteenth century, and has since remained the peculiar glory of the Anglican Church. Probably the best representative of the theological opinions of the earlier "Latitude" men was Archbishop Tillotson. By the eloquence and persuasiveness of his preaching, his great popularity and his undoubted piety, as well as from his supremely important position, he was soon regarded as the leader of this liberal school of thought. Tillotson, in common with all the Latitudinarians, placed special importance on bringing religion to the test of reason. "Christianity," he said, "is the best and the holiest, the wisest and most reasonable religion in the world," [1] and "all the precepts of it are reasonable and wise, requiring such duties as are suitable to the light of nature and do approve themselves to the best reason of mankind." [2] On these grounds he endeavoured to prove the *unreasonableness* of atheism and infidelity. In accordance with this principle he deprecated the study of those Divine mysteries which lay outside the province of reason, and preferred to concentrate his attention on the practical side of the Christian faith. He was pre-eminently a preacher of righteousness, and dwelt far more on positive moral duties than on definite Christian doctrines. "I hope that Jesus Christ is truly preached whenever His will and the laws and duties enjoined by the Christian religion are inculcated upon us." [3] This was perhaps a natural reaction from the precise and over-emphasised dogmatism of the Puritans, but it failed altogether to realise that the truest incentive to holiness and the cultivation of a virtuous life spring from a right appreciation of distinctive Christian doctrines, such as a firm faith in the atoning work of Christ and the power of His resurrection. This tendency to dwell exclusively on the practical conduct of everyday life became even more conspicuous in the eighteenth century, when all religion which approached the mysterious was deprecated and William Law was regarded as an unpractical mystic for insisting that the mysteries of Christian redemption were beyond the reach of human reasoning.

Tillotson pleaded for a full and free inquiry on all doctrines; every man should exercise his inalienable right to examine and

[1] Serm. v., Works, i. 448 (1820). [2] Serm. xlii., Works, iii. 275.
[3] Birch, *Life of Tillotson*, p. 28 (1753).

inquire freely into the grounds and reasons of his religion. "If your religion," he said, "be too good to be examined, I doubt if it is not too bad to be believed."[1] This contention was but in effect the logical outcome of the struggle for the right of private judgment which had been fought out at the Reformation, but hitherto had been mainly restricted to deciding matters of discipline and Church polity and had scarcely touched fundamental Christian doctrines. Tillotson was, however, wise enough to see the dangers which are involved in an unqualified exercise of private judgment, and thus he carefully defined its limits. A private person, he said, must not impose his judgment on others, and the right he possesses does not dispense with the necessity of guides and teachers in religion nor with due submission to authority; many people are too ignorant to judge of controverted questions, and should therefore not engage in religious disputes, but beg God's direction and rely on their teachers.[2]

It had been well if these wise cautions had been more carefully adhered to by Tillotson's successors in the eighteenth century, for Latitudinarian teaching tended to become more and more indefinite and unorthodox, largely owing to a radical fault in its theology. For it advocated too utilitarian a spirit in the cultivation of a religious life; holiness, virtue, and morality were inculcated rather on the grounds of prudence and a careful regard for happiness in this life and the next than from their inherent beauty. A modern Church historian has well remarked that "after the first ten or fifteen years of the century the Broad Church party in the Church of England was in no very satisfactory state. It had lost not only in spirit and energy, but also in earnestness and piety. Hoadly, Herring, Watson, Blackburne, all showed the characteristic defect of their age—a want of spiritual depth and fervour."[3]

Unfortunately, however, the method of opposition to this Broad Church teaching did little credit to the champions of orthodoxy. The Latitudinarian teachers were generally reviled by their High Church opponents with most opprobrious epithets. Even Tillotson was accused by Dean Hickes of being an "atheist."[4] Those who presumed to question the grounds of their faith, even when actuated by the sincere desire of solving

[1] Serm. lviii., Works, iv. 84. [2] *Cf.* Serm. xxi., Works, ii. 264–6.
[3] Abbey and Overton, *Eng. Ch. in 18th Cent.*, p. 113.
[4] Swift's Works, vol. xxiv., 1776. (Collin's *Discourse on Free-thinking.*)

doubts or difficulties, were relegated to the ranks of Deists and freethinkers. This general ostracism and wholesale condemnation must often have driven many honest inquirers to take refuge in Unitarianism or Deism. But although this uncharitable treatment was most injudicious, there were, it must be remembered, very real causes for alarm in this liberal theology.

Probably the most conspicuous example of its dangerous tendencies was the movement which was started to dispense with the subscription to the Articles of Religion. From quite early in the century there had been a radical difference of opinion amongst the Latitudinarians on this question. Many who were unable to endorse fully the Church's Confession of Faith regarded the required subscription to the Articles as a mere formality, testifying to their general acceptance of Church principles. There was, however, a numerous section which considered that this attitude savoured of dishonesty, and consequently desired a freedom from this binding test of orthodoxy, in order to advocate conscientiously their own special opinions. It is painfully evident that a great many clergy, whose views seriously diverged from the doctrines of the Church, under some specious pretext subscribed a full declaration of belief in her Articles. "Open or suspected Deists and Arians were known to have signed the Articles on the ground of general conformity to the English Church. . . . Arian subscription had become a familiar name." [1]

We must, however, remember that until 1865 a specific subscription "that all and every the Articles were agreeable to the Word of God" was required, instead of the more general declaration, in force now, that the doctrine of the Articles and Liturgy is agreeable to the Scriptures. It was also strongly argued at this time that the Articles, being compiled at a time when Calvinism was everywhere in the ascendant, were definitely of that complexion, whereas the vast majority of Anglican divines, owing to the movement in the last century headed by Archbishop Laud, held Arminian views, and therefore were forced to use a wide latitude in their interpretation of the Articles. A similar freedom was therefore claimed for those whose opinions inclined towards Arianism, and many of the clergy openly began to advocate Arian teaching alleging that their position was perfectly consistent with their solemn assent to the Church's doctrines. Dr. Samuel Clarke, who had narrowly escaped the

[1] *Eng. Ch. in 18th Cent.*, p. 193.

condemnation of Convocation in 1714 for his Arian tendencies, argued that "every person may reasonably agree to forms imposed by Protestant communities whenever he can in any sense at all reconcile them with Scripture." [1] Clarke soon put these principles into practice by actually publishing a reformed Church Prayer Book which included several alterations in an anti-Trinitarian direction. A number of clergy of extreme Latitudinarian views were not slow to follow this lead, and in 1746 a book was published by an incumbent named John Jones, advocating a thorough review of the teaching of the Established Church with a view "to remove such things as in the opinion of the wisest and best men the Church itself could ever boast of are inconsistent with true Protestant principles and greatly prejudicial to the interests of religion and virtue." [2] This book created much comment and met with great favour from many of the bishops and leading clergy, several of whom at this time undoubtedly sympathised with Arian opinions. The Primate, Archbishop Herring, had actually approved of Clarke's revised Prayer Book, and Bishop Sherlock thought it necessary to apologise to a Nonconformist minister for the retention of the Athanasian Creed; while Bishop Clayton of Clogher, in an *Essay on Spirit* in 1750, demanded its excision and advocated a general review of the Liturgy and the abolition of subscription to the Articles. In 1754 Archdeacon Blackburne, the champion of the Anti-Subscription party, seconded this demand in a letter written to the Primate, in which he pleaded that the removal of all subscription tests would be the most effectual means to counteract the deplorable immorality of the times.

In 1766 Blackburne published the *Confessional*, in which he forcibly exposed the hollowness of the mere general assent to Church principles which the Latitudinarian subscription involved, and vehemently opposed the excessive breadth of interpretation of such a view. He objected to the claim of churches to impose Confessions of Faith or "to attempt to settle religion once for all in an uncontrollable form" as an interference with the rights of individual Christians to search the Scriptures for themselves. "For where is there one of these Confessions," he asks, "which does not contain some very material decisions from which an intelligent Christian who hath duly examined the Scriptures may reasonably dissent?" [3]

[1] Waterland's Works, vol. i. p. 35 (1843). [2] *Monthly Review*, 1, 198.
[3] Blackburne's *Confessional*, pp. 32–4 (1767).

The Primate (Secker) strongly opposed these views, and they were specially obnoxious both to High Churchmen and Evangelicals, who detected in them, only too clearly, dangerous tendencies towards Socinianism and infidelity. Secker was, however, succeeded in the Primacy in 1768 by Archbishop Cornwallis, a mere courtier burdened with no orthodox scruples, and this change gave a further stimulus to the movement to abolish subscription, which now assumed a definite character. Blackburne organised meetings of sympathisers at the Feathers Tavern in the Strand, and in 1771 it was decided to draw up a Petition to Parliament for the removal of the tests. "The petitioners," it asserted, "have a natural right, and are also warranted by the original principles of the Reformation from Popery on which the Church of England is constituted, to judge in searching the Scriptures what may or may not be proved thereby." They claimed that the laws in regard to subscription to the Articles largely deprived them of this privilege, and therefore they prayed "that they may be relieved from such an imposition upon their judgments and be restored to their undoubted rights as Protestants of interpreting the Scriptures for themselves, without being bound by any human explications thereof, or required to acknowledge by subscription or declaration the truth of any formulary whatsoever beside Holy Scripture itself." [1]

This extravagant claim for an unlimited use of private judgment showed how far many of the later Latitudinarians had departed from the carefully defined limits to liberty of inquiry laid down by Archbishop Tillotson. Although this Petition was very widely circulated, only about two hundred and fifty signatures were obtained, and many of these were avowed Deists and Arians. Several orthodox clergymen, however, signed it, and it received the approval of both Watson and Paley. It was rejected by large majorities in Parliament for three successive years, and Edmund Burke used his eloquence to ridicule the grievances of which it complained. "They want," he said, "to be preferred clergymen of the Church of England as by law established, but their consciences will not allow them to conform to the doctrines and practices of that Church, that is, they want to be teachers in a church to which they do not belong, and to receive the emoluments appropriated for teaching one set of doctrines while they are teaching another; this is an odd sort of hardship." [2]

[1] *Parl. Hist.*, vol. xvii. pp. 251–2 (1813).
[2] Ibid., p. 280.

The failure of this Petition caused the secession of several clergy to the ranks of the Unitarians.

A further attempt was made for the revision of the Liturgy and for a modification of the subscription test, by a proposal that only the Articles relating to fundamental doctrines should be subscribed. This effort, although supported by Beilby Porteus, afterwards Bishop of London, came to nothing, the Bishops apparently considering it wiser to adopt Walpole's policy of "quieta non movere" and "let sleeping dogs lie."

CHAPTER IV

"CONTROVERSIES OF FAITH"

It is not surprising that, with the alarming growth of Latitudinarian principles, constant, subtle, and determined attacks were made against the main doctrines of the Christian revelation, and thus the eighteenth century was largely occupied with theological and philosophical controversies. It has been well remarked that "after Queen Anne's reign the main interest of English Church history rests for a time on the religious thought of the age rather than on its practice."[1] The intellectual powers of divines were thoroughly tested in their struggle to defend the cause of orthodoxy; but they were more than equal to the task, and their brilliant literary achievements have furnished succeeding generations of Churchmen with an invaluable storehouse for the defence of the Catholic faith. The silencing of Convocation in 1717 had enabled the clergy to express their opinions with greater impunity, as they were removed from the danger of official condemnation by the recognised synods of the Church. But the commencement of the Trinitarian Controversy dated back long before this time. It may be said to have arisen after the publication in 1685 of Bishop Bull's celebrated treatise *Defensio Fidei Nicænæ*. This was a most scholarly, but purely historical, work, mainly occupied with discovering the exact views of the Ante-Nicene Fathers on the Trinity, and more especially on the relation of the Son to the Father. Bull conclusively proved that, in spite of many indefinite

[1] *Eng. Ch. in 18th Cent.*, p. 20.

statements made by the Early Fathers, the fundamental doctrine of the consubstantiality of the Son with the Father was thoroughly warranted by Ante-Nicene teaching.

After the Revolution, disputes on the Catholic doctrine of the Trinity became very frequent, and many treatises were written in defence and explanation of the orthodox faith. Sherlock in his *Vindication of the Trinity*, in attempting to give a reasonable explanation of the mystery, narrowly bordered on Tritheism, while South, his opponent, went to the other extreme of Sabellianism. So fierce did the controversy become that in 1696 Royal Injunction forbade any teaching on the subject not in accordance with the Church's doctrinal formulæ. In spite of this prohibition the disputes continued, and in the eighteenth century, when all doctrines were being brought to the supreme test of "reason," the attacks on the Trinity became bolder, and were concerned not merely with its mode of definition, but with the truth of the doctrine itself. William Whiston, a learned Cambridge professor but a most eccentric individual, published a book called *Primitive Christianity Revived*,[1] in which, while repudiating Arianism, he endeavoured to expose the errors of the orthodox view of the Trinity, or what he termed the "Athanasian heresy." He called himself a "Eusebian," and pleaded for the recognition of the "Apostolical Canons and Constitutions" (generally considered forgeries) as "the most sacred of the canonical books of the New Testament." But being strictly honest, eventually he came to the conclusion that his position as a Churchman was inconsistent, and he ended his days amongst the general Baptists. He had, however, collected around him a number of sympathisers who largely shared his opinions. The most famous of these was his great friend Dr. Samuel Clarke, who became the foremost champion of Arian views. He was a divine of high repute and great ability, and was Royal Chaplain successively to William III, Anne, George I., and George II. In 1712 he published his *Scripture Doctrine of the Trinity*, in which he had collected no less than 1251 texts in the New Testament bearing on the nature of the Godhead. His conclusions were that the one supreme God is the Father, and that the Son is only divine so far as the Father is able to communicate divinity, while the Holy Spirit is inferior in dominion and authority both to the Father and the Son. He maintained that worship of a higher nature is due to God the Father than that due to Christ, and that the Son is

[1] See p. 16.

subordinate in authority and dominion to the Father. Dr. Clarke and his followers strongly urged that these views were not inconsistent with the teaching of the Church Liturgy and Articles.

These opinions were soon vigorously opposed by a large number of writers, all of whom, however, sink into insignificance when compared with the exhaustive and comprehensive treatises of Daniel Waterland, who exposed so thoroughly the hopeless inconsistency of Clarke's position that it has seldom been occupied since. Waterland had spent most of his life at Cambridge, first as Fellow, then as Master of Magdalene College. He was a most profound scholar and a very clear and logical writer. He was especially well acquainted with the writings of the Early Fathers, to which he constantly appealed. He, however, carefully defined the value and authority of Patristic writings, declaring that they afforded clear evidence of contemporary Church doctrine and a good probability of what that doctrine had been from the beginning, but their testimony was of no weight if it was plainly contrary to Scripture. "As to authority," he affirms, "in a strict and proper sense, I do not know that the fathers have any over us; they are all dead men; therefore we urge not their authority but their testimony, their judgment as carrying great force of reason with it, and reason we should all submit to. I follow the fathers as far as reason requires and no further."[1] His great work, *A Vindication of Christ's Divinity*, was published in 1719. He challenged the position adopted by Clarke at every point, and courageously dealt with the undoubted difficulties involved in the deep mystery of the Trinity. He boldly charges Clarke and his followers with falling into polytheism. "You are Tritheists in the same sense as Pagans are called Polytheists. One supreme and two inferior Gods is your avowed doctrine; that is, three Gods. . . . Scripture and antiquity generally say nothing of a supreme God because they acknowledge no inferior God. Such language was borrowed from Pagans and then used by Christian writers. So too was the notion of 'mediatorial worship' borrowed from the Pagans, handed on by Arians, and brought down to our own times by Papists." In reply to the repudiation of Arianism made by Clarke's party on the ground that they did not make Christ a creature, Waterland said: "You assert, though not directly, yet consequentially, that the Maker and Redeemer of the whole world is no more than a creature, that He depends entirely upon the favour and good pleasure of

[1] Works, vol. i. 96 (1843).

God. . . . There is no middle between being essentially a God and being a creature."

In regard to the mysteriousness of the doctrine of the Trinity, Waterland well says: "The Omnipresence, the Incarnation, Self-existence, are all mysteries, and Eternity itself the greatest mystery of all. There is nothing peculiar in the Trinity that is near so perplexing as Eternity." [1]

But although the Church owes such a great debt to Waterland for his defence of the Trinity, he is better remembered to-day for his invaluable treatise *A Review of the Doctrine of the Eucharist*, which deserves to rank with the writings of Hooker and Pearson as a standard work on the doctrinal position of the Anglican Church. It is a work, as his biographer Bishop Van Mildert well said, "of established reputation both here and abroad, for which he had been collecting materials during a considerable portion of his life." [2] Occasioned largely by a contemporary treatise called the *Unbloody Sacrifice* and by Bishop Hoadly's *Plain Account of the Nature and End of the Sacrament of the Lord's Supper*, published at this time, Waterland proved conclusively, by copious references to the writings of the Fathers of the first four centuries, that the Church of England taught the true Catholic view of the Sacrament of the Lord's Supper as against the Romanists on the one hand and the Lutherans or Socinians on the other. Against the Romish contention he well says: "To say that the Communion of our Lord's body and blood means the receiving of His natural flesh and blood into our mouths, under the forms, accidents, or appearances of bread and wine, is manifestly a forced and late interpretation; not heard of for eight hundred years or more, and besides absurd, contradictory, and impossible . . . the bread and wine do remain, after consecration, the same in substance as before, changed only as to their uses, relations, or offices . . . The symbolical body and blood (bread and wine) are there present, the rest is present only in a figure or under certain construction." Against the Lutheran view he says: "To say that the Communion signifies the eating Christ's glorified body by faith, is not a just interpretation . . . because what is represented and eaten in the Sacrament is not the body glorified, but the body crucified and blood shed, which are no more, and therefore cannot be received either with mouth or mind, excepting only in a qualified and

[1] *Cf.* vols. i., ii., and iii. of Waterland's Works.
[2] *Life of Waterland*, Works, i. 168 (1856).

figurative sense." Yet Waterland was equally clear in his repudiation of the idea of a bare commemoration, and while explaining that the use of the term "real presence" is nowhere authorised by the formularies of the Church, he admits that "the term seems to be grounded on Scripture," for though there is no corporal presence, yet there is a spiritual one exhibitive of Divine blessings and graces, and though we eat not Christ's natural glorified body in the Sacrament, or out of it, yet our mystical union with that very body is strengthened and perfected in and through the Sacrament by the operation of the Holy Spirit."[1] It had been well if this clear, full, yet moderate teaching had been more closely adhered to by divines emphasising either the "Catholic" or "Protestant" aspect of the Church.

The writings of Dr. Clarke on the Trinity had not only affected Church of England divines, but were the occasion of a fierce dispute amongst the Nonconformist bodies. The Arian doctrines proclaimed by two Dissenting ministers at Exeter caused such alarm that a Conference was held at Salters' Hall in London, in 1719, where the majority agreed to an orthodox definition of the Trinity. A large number of the Presbyterians and some of the Baptists still adhered to their Arian tenets, and by degrees, realising their untenable position, they drifted into Unitarianism. Dr. Lardner, one of the most celebrated of these divines, plainly stated that "Jesus Christ was a mere man with whom God was, in a peculiar and extraordinary manner." The Independents, however, remained true to the orthodox doctrine of the Trinity, and their celebrated divine Isaac Watts, the well-known hymn-writer, wrote a valuable and popular defence called a *Treatise on the Christian Doctrine of the Trinity*.

The very unorthodox opinions of Bishop Clayton on the Trinity, which appeared in his *Essay on Spirit*, were the occasion of a very able treatise by William Jones of Nayland, who maintained that every article of the Christian faith depended on the Catholic doctrine of the Trinity. In 1782 the controversy was again revived under the more consistent form of Unitarianism by the writings of a clever scientist, Dr. Priestley, but his *History of the Corruptions of Christianity* was ably refuted by Bishop Horsley.

It is impossible in so short a space to give more than a bare outline of the important Deistic movement, which, although not so widespread, created even more excitement than the Trinitarian

[1] *Doctrine of Eucharist*, pp. 171–80 (1868).

controversy with which it synchronised. The Deists organised no party, and were merely a collection of individual writers of no special literary genius, possessing no uniform creed or doctrine, and agreeing only in their general opinions and method of argument. Their cardinal principle was the substitution of reason for authority in matters of religion. "It was an attempt," says Dr. Spooner, "to assert the claims of reason against those of faith."[1] Their main concern was to discover the method of God's revelation to man, and their general solution of this problem was that God has so plainly revealed Himself to mankind by His works in Nature that there is no need of a further or better revelation. Their great contention was, therefore, that man should follow the light of nature which a supreme Being had implanted within him. The earlier writers professed their attachment to the National Church, their sincere intention of defending the Christian religion, and their respect for Revelation, but most of the later Deists discredited the latter, even if they did not altogether reject it as out of harmony with reason. In its origin the movement seems to have been an attempt to escape from the bitter theological strife, so marked a feature of the seventeenth century, by an appeal to a natural religion. They professed to follow in the footsteps of the philosopher John Locke, who, however, distinctly dissociated himself from their opinions.

Locke in his *Essay on Human Understanding*, published towards the end of the previous century, had asserted that Revelation cannot be admitted against the plain evidence of reason—"a man," he said, "can admit nothing to be true in direct contradiction to the clear evidence of his own understanding"[2]—but yet he allowed that certain truths which are above our reason should be accepted on the faith of Revelation. "Whatever proposition is revealed of whose truth our mind by its natural faculties and notions cannot judge, that is purely a matter of faith and above reason."[2] He limits the province of reason to testing the evidence for a genuine revelation.

Although Locke's *Reasonableness of Christianity* was written expressly against Deism, yet it met with much censure in orthodox circles. His main object was to present the most rational form of religion, and thus he objected to the enforcement of particular creeds or to any Church authority in religious matters. His idea of faith was confined to a simple belief in Jesus as the Messiah,

[1] *Life of Butler*, p. 128.
[2] Book iv. chap. 18, pp. 585 and 588 (1875).

asserting that His miracles were a conclusive proof of this claim. "A Christian I am sure I am, because I believe Jesus to be the Messiah, the King and Saviour promised and sent by God."[1] Although he was of an essentially pious and reverent disposition, and in regard to Revelation such a distinct opponent of rationalism that he stated, "The Bible is God's Word, and every word of it ought to be believed by every Christian man,"[1] yet in so far as he was an apostle of human reason as opposed to human authority he laid the foundation on which the Deists built.

Thus in 1696 appeared a book which created immense excitement, called *Christianity not Mysterious*, written by John Toland, an ex-Romanist. He stated that his purpose was "to make it appear that the use of reason was not so dangerous in religion as is commonly represented."[2] He maintained that nothing in the Gospel was contrary to reason or above it, and that no Christian doctrine is really a mystery. Although he is very careful in the application of this theory, yet the tendency of his views is to undermine Revelation, as he aims at dispensing with what he calls "unreasonable" accretions to Christianity. In his conclusion he states: "I am fully convinced that there is no Mystery in Christianity, and by consequence nothing contradictory or inconceivable, however made an article of faith, can be contained in the Gospels, if it be really the Word of God . . . whatever instance can be alleged (to the contrary) must either be found not *mysterious*, or, if it prove a Mystery, not divinely revealed."

Another book which occasioned almost as much opposition as Toland's was Anthony Collins's *Discourse on Freethinking*, published in 1713. He urged that the verdict of free inquiry into theological questions had always been adverse to supernaturalism. The answer of Bentley, although marred by somewhat abusive language, was generally supposed to have shown the fallacy of Collins's contention. In 1726, however, Collins published a far more serious attack on Christianity in his *Discourse on the Grounds and Reasons of the Christian Religion*, in which he endeavoured to prove that the truth of Christianity depended on the fulfilment of Old Testament prophecies concerning the Messiah, and was not affected by any miracles or authority of the New Testament. He then proceeded to discredit the evidential value of prophecies by asserting that they

[1] Locke's Works, vi. 351 and 359 (1824). [2] Preface, p. vii. (1702).

were never fulfilled except in an allegorical sense. Although this work met with the strongest opposition, it was soon followed by a far more extravagant attack on the Miracles by Thomas Woolston. In his *Six Discourses on the Miracles of our Saviour*, written in a most profane and blasphemous spirit, he treats the miracles as mere allegories, and ridicules the idea of their literal interpretation. His wild theories were ably refuted by Thomas Sherlock's *Tryal of the Witnesses of the Resurrection of Jesus*.

The Deistical work, however, which created the greatest sensation was Matthew Tindal's *Christianity as old as the Creation*, which appeared in 1730. It takes up the definite position of frank hostility to Christianity which was followed by practically all the later Deistic writers. Tindal argued that any external Revelation was not only incredible but altogether superfluous and useless, because "the original law and religion of nature is so perfect that nothing can possibly be added to it by any subsequent external revelation whatsoever."[1] "What impartial man," he asks, "can find from all the conduct of Christians that they arrive to any higher state of perfection than the rest of mankind who are supposed to continue in their degeneracy and corruption?"[2] "If," he argues, "God's ways are equal, how can we suppose he left all mankind for so many ages in a most miserable state of doubt and uncertainty about the pardon of sin, and consequently about the possibility of any man's being saved?"[3]

Although the Deistic controversy was still continued by such writings as those of Morgan and Chubb, Tindal's book was generally regarded as a standard work and as a final and complete definition of the Deistic position. These later Deistic works, especially Tindal's, brought forth a perfect host of answers, the most celebrated of which were Bishop Warburton's *Divine Legation of Moses* and Bishop Berkeley's fascinating treatise, *Alciphron; or, the Minute Philosopher*, while Nonconformists such as Chandler, Doddridge, and Leland ably championed the cause of Christianity. It must, however, be sufficient here to give a short account of what may well be described as the theological masterpiece of the century—Bishop Butler's famous *Analogy of Religion*, published in 1736. Starting on the central Deistic assumption of a wise and intelligent moral Governor of the world, Butler presents the whole case for Christianity as a complete system, and although professing to answer no special Deistic writer, he yet suggests and

[1] Leland's *View of Deistical Writers*, i. 149 (1754).
[2] *Christianity as old as the Creation*, p. 366 (1730). [3] Ibid., p. 380.

answers all their real objections in a candid, comprehensive, and masterly manner. "He told a friend that his way of writing it had been to endeavour to answer as he went along every possible objection that might occur to any one against any position of his in his book." [1] "The *Analogy*," it has been well said, "furnishes a sort of summary of the Deistical controversy. There is probably not a single argument advanced on the Deistical side which Butler has not pondered, and to which he has not furnished something of an answer." [2] He fully admits the use of reason "as the only faculty we have to judge concerning anything, even Revelation itself." [3] "Let reason," he says in another place, "be kept to, and if any part of the Scripture account of the redemption of the world by Christ can be shown to be really contrary to it, let the Scripture, in the name of God, be given up; but let not such poor creatures as we go on objecting against an infinite scheme that we do not see the necessity or usefulness of all its parts, and call this reasoning." [4] But he constantly shows the limitations of merely human knowledge, and he possessed a full realisation of God's greatness and man's insignificance.

The work was the result of twenty years' study and reflection, and the main aim is to prove from the facts of daily experience an analogy between what the Deists called Natural Religion and the religion unfolded to us by Revelation, and to show that there are the same difficulties and objections to be found in the one as in the other, and that therefore the special doctrines of Christianity are neither improbable nor unreasonable, and ought not to be lightly rejected. "The design," he says, "of the following treatise will be to show that the several parts principally objected against in this moral, and Christian dispensation including its scheme, its publication, and the proof which God has afforded us of its truth; that the particular parts objected to in this whole dispensation are analogous to what is experienced in the constitution and course of Nature, or Providence. . . . This argument from analogy is in general unanswerable and undoubtedly of weight on the side of religion, notwithstanding the objection which may seem to be against it. . . . And I shall begin it with that which is the foundation of all our hopes and of all our fears, which are of any consideration, I mean in a future life." [5]

[1] Bartlett's *Memoir of Butler*, p. 50 (1839).
[2] Spooner, *Life of Butler*, p. 126.
[3] *Analogy*, Part II. chap. iii. p. 182 (R.T.S.).
[4] Ibid., Part II. chap. v. p. 226. [5] Ibid., Introduction, p. 12.

In dealing with Natural Religion, Butler insists that mankind is appointed to live in a future state, where he will be rewarded or punished in accordance with his virtuous or vicious behaviour here, and that our present life is a probation and state of trial and discipline for a future one, and that the objections urged against this doctrine are not valid. In reviewing revealed religion, he urges that the state of sin and apostasy in which the world is, furnished an occasion for an additional dispensation of providence which is of the utmost importance, proved by miracles, but containing in it many strange and unexpected things, and is a system for the recovery of the world carried on by the mediation of a Divine person, the Messiah, and only revealed to such part of mankind, and with such particular evidence, as the wisdom of God thought fit. In his concluding remarks Butler claims that his treatise " will be to such as are convinced of religion upon the proof arising out of liberty and moral fitness an additional proof and confirmation of it, and to such as do not admit these principles an original proof of it. Those who believe will here find the scheme of Christianity cleared of objections, and the evidence of it in a peculiar manner strengthened; those who do not believe will at least be shown the absurdity of all attempts to prove Christianity false, the plain undoubted credibility of it, and I hope a good deal more."[1]

It is probable that Butler's great work contributed in no small measure to the failure of the Deistic movement, which had completely collapsed by the middle of the century. The Deists had entirely failed to realise the ignorance and perversion of man's reason, and therefore they denied the moral utility of Revelation. The collapse of the movement was, however, due to the fact that it did not go far enough. It was an illogical attempt to substitute for Christianity a religion of Nature, and thus became a sort of half-way house between Christianity and atheism. In the latter half of the century a more consistent position was adopted in the undisguised sceptical and infidel attacks which were made on the Christian faith. The writings of Lord Shaftesbury, published early in the century, although agreeing in the main with the Deistic position, had treated the Christian faith in such a cynical and sarcastic manner that Pope asserted that " they had done more harm to revealed religion in England than all the works of Infidelity put together."[2] But the posthumous works

[1] *Analogy*, p. 300.

[2] *Warburton and Hurd's Letters*, Letter xvii., p. 36 (1809).

of Lord Bolingbroke, which appeared in 1754, went a step further in the sceptical direction. Besides openly rejecting distinctive Christian doctrines such as the Trinity and the Atonement, he violently assailed the teaching of St. Paul, the credibility of the Gospel story, and even criticised the character of Christ.

The first writer of any note, however, who openly attacked the very foundations of Natural as well as Revealed religion was David Hume, who published in 1750 his *Philosophical Essays concerning Human Understanding*. Basing his religious opinions upon his somewhat conflicting philosophical principles, he launched his famous thesis against the possibility of miracles. He contended that miracles were impossible because they contradicted the universal testimony to the uniformity of Nature, and that no alleged miracle had sufficient evidence for its support. Hume, however, failed to recognise that the uniformity of nature is merely a general assumption which it is not possible to prove except by an imperfect inductive method. His argument was fully answered by Leland, in his *View of Deistical Writers*, who pointed out that the truth of a miracle rested on the genuineness of the New Testament writings, the evidential value of which was so ably demonstrated by Paley a few years later.

But probably a far more dangerous blow was aimed at Christianity by the learned and fascinating historical work of Edward Gibbon, published in 1776. The 15th and 16th chapters of the *Decline and Fall of the Roman Empire* contained a thinly veiled attack on the divine character of Christianity. The merely human reasons which are alleged to account for its rapid growth, the base motives of superstition or self-interest which are attributed to the early converts, the elaborate attempt to reduce the number of the Christian martyrs or to attribute their sufferings to misdirected zeal, as well as the abundant sarcasm which is employed in describing the severe and ascetic morality of some of the early Christians, were all calculated to do far more harm to the cause of true religion than any open attack on the Christian faith. Gibbon's writings had appealed to the cultured and educated classes, but Thomas Paine's *Age of Reason*, which appeared in 1794, was a blatant attempt to unsettle the faith of the humbler and more ignorant. It was written in a most blasphemous style, pouring contempt and abuse on the Holy Scriptures. Both Gibbon and Paine were, however, well refuted by Paley in his classic work the *Evidences of Christianity*, and by Bishop Watson in his *Apology for Christianity*, which appeared in 1776, and his *Apology for the Bible*, published in 1796.

Dangerous and disturbing as these controversies and attacks on the Christian faith were at the time, the Church had no cause to regret them afterwards. Instead of permanently harming her, they rather strengthened her position and vindicated her orthodoxy, showing that it was proof against all assaults both from within and without. They had been specially fruitful in exposing some of the mistaken lines of defence adopted by apologists for the faith, and consequently had compelled theologians to re-adjust their arguments to meet the problems of a new philosophy. "By clearing away much dead matter they had prepared the way for a reconstruction of theology from the very depths of the heart's beliefs." [1]

CHAPTER V

THE HANOVERIAN BISHOPS AND CLERGY

WITH the growth of scepticism and infidelity in the country and the spread of Deistic and unorthodox opinions amongst Churchmen, it is not surprising to find that the leading clergy of the Hanoverian period were not conspicuous for the piety of their lives or for an arduous devotion to their pastoral duties. In the early years of the century the Church had possessed a number of bishops and eminent divines who for their practical piety, ability, and activity would have been a credit to any age, but as the century advanced the current problems and controversies of the day produced a marked change for the worse in the character of the prominent ecclesiastics. The intellectual and theological controversies which were raging with such acrimony so largely occupied the attention of the bishops and clergy that in a great measure the practical and more immediate responsibilities of the diocese and the parish were neglected. The pens of the theologians and Christian apologists were well employed, but too often this work was substituted for the more urgent need of restraining the vice and impiety of the age and of evangelising the careless and unconverted. This controversial spirit was not, however, by any means mainly responsible for

[1] J. A. Dorner, *History of Prot. Theology*, ii. 77 (1871).

the deplorable deterioration in character and usefulness which was so marked a feature of the clergy, and especially of the bishops, of this period. For while carefully avoiding the extreme statements and sweeping assertions which have been too often made concerning the Hanoverian clergy, it is impossible to deny that many of the bishops were excessively worldly, culpably idle and negligent, and too often mere self-seeking political partisans. It is true that their faults and failings, although inexcusable, were largely the result of the conditions of the times in which they lived, yet even those who rose superior to the spirit of the age by their exemplary lives, learning, and energy were unable to offer any effective check to the growing demoralisation of society.

A very large share of the blame for the degenerate condition of the Georgian clergy must fall on the ecclesiastical policy pursued by the State. Not only had Convocation been silenced, but, as we have already noticed, from the commencement of George I.'s reign Church patronage had been bestowed almost entirely on men of Whig sympathies and Latitudinarian views. Walpole regarded the disposal of ecclesiastical preferment as a valuable means of further establishing his own power; while Lord Chancellor Hardwicke "thought it his duty to dispose of the ecclesiastical preferments in his gift with a view to increase his own political influence, without any scrupulous regard for the interests of religion, and without the slightest respect for scientific or literary merit." [1] Even Dr. Johnson, who was second to none in his affection and jealous regard for the honour and interests of the Church, admits that "no man can now be made a bishop for his learning and piety, his only chance is his being connected with some one who has parliamentary interest." [2] As late as 1764 Grenville classified bishoprics as of two kinds—"those of business for men of abilities and learning, and those of ease for men of family and fashion." Thus the great majority of the bishops were appointed because of their political influence or connection with the dominant Whig interest. Bishop Watson says he received the see of Llandaff from Lord Shelburne in 1782 because he thought that "I was a warm and might become a useful partisan." [3]

The result of this disastrous policy was that the higher offices

[1] Campbell's *Lives of the Chancellors*, vol. vi. p. 298 (1857).
[2] Boswell's *Life of Johnson*, vol. i. p. 558 (edn. Everyman's Library).
[3] *Anecdotes of Life of Bp. Watson*, i. 94 (1817).

of the Church were soon filled by men whose main object in life seemed to consist in gaining the favour of the minister in office with a view to securing some much-coveted "prize" of Church patronage. Bishop Watson tells us: "I saw the generality of the Bishops bartering their independence and dignity of their order for the chance of a translation, and polluting Gospel humility by the pride of prelacy."[1] Pluralities and non-residence were common; even the best of the bishops thought it no disgrace to hold two or three important and lucrative posts at the same time, while others, who were well provided for, still urged that their merits had been insufficiently rewarded, and in a most shamelessly mendicant spirit poured their grievances into the ears of powerful statesmen. The extent to which this degrading custom was carried is well illustrated by the appeal made to the Duke of Newcastle in 1761 by Bishop Newton, who wrote: "I think it my duty to acquaint your Grace that the Archbishop of York lies a-dying and, as all here think, cannot possibly live beyond to-morrow morning, if so long. Upon this occasion of two vacancies, I beg, I hope, I trust your Grace's kindness and goodness will be shown to one who has long solicited your favour."[2] Important positions seem to have been undertaken solely on account of the pecuniary advantages accruing from them, and with but little idea of the responsibilities involved. Probably no better example of glaring disregard of duty can be found than the case of Bishop Watson of Llandaff, who rarely ever visited his diocese, and although he did notable service to Christianity by his apologetical writings, yet boasted that he spent his time in field diversions and farming in the North of England, alleging that by such occupation he had "set an example of spirited husbandry and honourably provided for his family."

Only a year after the accession of George I. the death of Archbishop Tenison caused a vacancy in the primacy, which was filled by the appointment of William Wake, who had just closed ten years of energetic work as Bishop of Lincoln. Distinguished both as a preacher and author, he took a keen interest in patristic studies, but he was first brought into prominence by his strenuous opposition to Atterbury's views on the Convocation question, and in 1703 he published a learned and exhaustive treatise on the history and power of the English Convocations. "He was a man eminently learned, an excellent writer, a good preacher, and, which

[1] *Anecdotes of Life of Bp. Watson*, p. 71.
[2] Quoted in Overton and Relton (*ante*), p. 160.

is above all, a man of an exemplary life." [1] He was conspicuous in an intolerant age for the liberality of his ecclesiastical views, and was a strong opponent of the narrow political type of churchmanship represented by Sacheverell. His tenure of the primacy was remarkable for the singular correspondence he conducted with a view to a union with the Gallican Church, mention of which will be made later. Ill-health compelled him to live much in retirement, and in his later years his duties largely devolved on Bishop Gibson of London. He died in 1737, and was succeeded by John Potter (1674–1747), a High Churchman of Whig sympathies and of pre-eminent scholarship. Even in his youth he had distinguished himself by his ability as an author, and his *Discourse of Church Government* was for many years a popular and highly valued theological work. He apparently saw no evil in "pluralism," as he continued to hold a rich living and a University professorship during his tenure of the see of Oxford (1715–27). Although sharing the common dread of "enthusiasm" in religion, he gave John Wesley some very practical advice which he fully profited by. "If you desire to be useful," he told Wesley, "do not spend your time and strength in contending for or against such things as are of a disputable nature, but in testifying against open, notorious vice and in promoting real essential holiness." [2] The son of a linendraper, his somewhat unexpected promotion to the most exalted position in the Church probably accounted for the extravagant view he took of the dignity and respect due to his important office, so that we are told that after he became Archbishop he was inordinately fond of official pomp and ceremony, and "would procure half a dozen footmen to walk bareheaded by him when he was in his coach, three of a side ; besides his train bearer." [3]

By far the most celebrated prelate of the eighteenth century was Joseph Butler, who on the death of Potter is reported to have declined the primacy on the ground that it was "too late to try to support a falling church." [4] The son of a well-to-do Presbyterian, he was educated at a Dissenting academy at Tewkesbury, and when only twenty-one showed proof of his later fame as a profound thinker by engaging in a deep metaphysical dispute with the famous Dr. Samuel Clarke, in which he declared "the search

[1] Tindal's *Rapin*, vol. iv. p. 435.
[2] Southey, *Life of Wesley*, p. 146 (Hutchinson).
[3] Whiston's Memoirs, p. 360 (1749).
[4] *Dict. Nat. Biog.*, article "Butler."

after truth to be the business of his life." [1] He was a supremely conscientious man of the deepest religious convictions, and his belief in God was no mere philosophical theory, but, as a recent biographer states, " God is for him a reality and the greatest of realities, a Being about whose existence it is as little possible to doubt as it is about one's own existence." [2] He was a great friend and favourite of Queen Caroline, who was charmed with his famous *Analogy*, written during his quiet retirement in the living of Stanhope. It was through her influence that he was offered and accepted the see of Bristol in 1738, but as this was only worth £400 a year he frankly informed Walpole that " it was not very suitable either to the condition of my fortune or the circumstances of my preferment, nor exactly what I might have expected from the Queen's recommendation." [3] He commenced his episcopal duties in a spirit little in harmony with the lax discipline of the times. He showed great care in his selection of ordination candidates, and exerted himself to prevent the evils of pluralities and non-residence. He is reported to have spent £4000 on the repair of the episcopal palace. He was, however, charged with " superstition " for erecting a cross of white marble underneath the east window of the palace chapel, and after his death a most unwarrantable and uncharitable assertion was made that he had died in communion with the Romish Church on the ground " that there was nothing improbable in it, when it is considered that the same prelate put up the popish insignia of the cross in his chapel when at Bristol, and in his last Episcopal charge had squinted very much towards that superstition." [4] He took a deep interest in the missionary work of the Society for the Propagation of the Gospel, but in spite of all his efforts he failed to remove the hostility of the Dissenters in the colonies to the creation of colonial bishoprics, as these descendants of the Puritans still preserved bitter memories of the persecuting zeal of Archbishop Laud. Butler was at first sympathetic with the Methodist movement, but he afterwards told Whitefield that " the pretending to extraordinary revelations and gifts of the Holy Ghost is a horrid thing, a very horrid thing." [5]

In 1750 he was translated to the rich see of Durham, and although most simple in his own mode of living, during the two

[1] Butler's Works, p. 299 (1841). [2] Spooner, *Life of Butler*, p. 53.
[3] Steere's Memoir of Bp. Butler, p. xxiii. (1862).
[4] Bartlett's *Memoir of Butler*, p. 153.
[5] *Dict. Nat. Biog.*, article " Butler."

years he was there he dispensed hospitality on a princely scale. A contemporary writer tells us that "during the short time he held the see he conciliated all hearts. In advanced years and on the episcopal throne, he retained the same genuine modesty and native sweetness of disposition which had distinguished him in youth. During the ministerial performance of the sacred office a divine animation seemed to pervade his whole manner and lighted up his pale wan countenance, already marked with the progress of disease, like a torch glimmering in its socket, but bright and useful to the last." [1]

The prelate who was held in almost universal esteem was Butler's lifelong friend, Martin Benson, who was made Bishop of Gloucester in 1735. Of great piety, and carefully avoiding controversy, he devoted himself entirely to his pastoral duties, and for seventeen years set an example of conscientious and energetic work, then all too rare. He did much to improve the condition of the clergy of his diocese, and he will always be affectionately remembered as the constant friend and patron of George Whitefield. An intimate friend of both Benson and Butler was Thomas Secker, who was appointed Bishop of Bristol in 1735, translated to Oxford two years later, and in 1758 succeeded to the primacy. He had been educated at the same Dissenting academy as Butler, and, largely owing to his influence, decided to enter the ministry of the Church in which he afterwards had such a distinguished career. Although he distinctly disapproved of the methods adopted by Wesley and Whitefield for a revival of true spiritual religion, he thoroughly appreciated their motives, as he described Wesley "as labouring to bring all the world to solid inward vital religion." [2] He took a most pessimistic view of the religious condition of the nation, publicly stating that "Christianity is now railed at and ridiculed with very little reason, and the teachers of it without any at all," and that "disregard to religion is become, through a variety of unhappy causes, the distinguishing character of the present age," [3] yet he had an intense dread of "enthusiasm," and his correct but cold Christianity did much to maintain the dead level of merely respectable orthodoxy which was so characteristic of and so harmful to the Church life of the eighteenth century. He died in 1768.

Probably the bishop who possessed the greatest power and

[1] Preface to *Analogy*, p. xi. (R.T.S.).
[2] *Dict. Nat. Biog.*, vol. lx. p. 310.
[3] *Eight Charges* (edit. 1780), pp. 4–5.

influence in high places was Edmund Gibson, who was in charge of the important see of London 1723–48. He was the trusted friend and ecclesiastical adviser of Walpole, although he probably sacrificed his chance of the primacy by his opposition to that all-powerful minister on a political question. Gibson was a voluminous writer, but not specially energetic in his diocese, although he did a good deal in a quiet way to restrain vice and impiety. He was succeeded by Thomas Sherlock (1678–1761), the son of the celebrated Dean Sherlock who had gained such unenviable notoriety in the last century by his sudden change of front on the Nonjuring question. Sherlock was very tolerant and liberal in his ecclesiastical views, and, like his father, a brilliant scholar and theologian. The "Bangorian Controversy" afforded him an opportunity of measuring his intellect with the famous Bishop Hoadly, whom he succeeded as Bishop of Bangor in 1727. He was removed to Salisbury in 1734, where he remained till he undertook the bishopric of London in 1749, the arduous duties of which his advancing age prevented him from carrying out in a very vigorous or active manner.

Probably no other age can furnish a better example of genuine self-sacrificing devotion to duty than the truly apostolic career of Thomas Wilson, who was for fifty-eight years bishop of the island diocese of Sodor and Man. His abundant zeal and undoubted piety, as well as the transparent simplicity and humility of his life, form a striking contrast to the lives of most of his contemporaries. Although his income was only £300 a year, he repeatedly refused the offer of a rich living to hold *in commendam*, while the tempting allurements of rich English bishoprics had no power to alienate him from the flock he loved so devotedly. Money he regarded only as a useful means of relieving the needs of others, and quite half his small income was devoted to charitable purposes. In his strenuous endeavours to extinguish wickedness and vice he exercised a rigorous penal discipline which would have been impossible in a less independent sphere, and was only fully suitable to more primitive conditions. Offending Christians were excommunicated and excluded from the society of the faithful, while those who refused to carry out the harsh and often humiliating penances imposed on them were summarily committed to prison till they came to a better mind. A woman of notoriously immoral life was actually sentenced to be dragged after a boat in the sea, and this outrageous punishment was duly carried out; with an apparently profitable result.

The clergy were treated with equal severity, and frequently suspended from their office for even minor offences. This severe discipline incurred the bitter opposition of those who had no spiritual sympathy with his aims, and in 1713 a collision with the civil authority led to the imprisonment of the Bishop for two months owing to his refusal to pay a fine. Wilson took a deep interest in foreign missionary effort, and in his own diocese he succeeded in establishing parochial schools, and often libraries, under the personal supervision of the clergy. His early studies in medicine he put to good use by gratuitously relieving the wants of the sick poor. His writings furnish abundant proof of his practical piety and true sympathy; his tract on the *Principles and Duties of Christianity* was the first book ever published in the Manx language. He died in 1755 at the great age of ninety-two.

Turning to the bishops of the reign of George III., we are at once introduced to the name of William Warburton, Bishop of Gloucester 1760–79, who probably surpassed all his contemporaries by his brilliant intellectual gifts and literary attainments. Chatham said that "nothing of a private nature had given him so much pleasure as bringing Dr. Warburton upon the Bench." [1] Dr. Johnson, alluding to his great reading, said: "His table is always full. He brings things from the north and the south and from every quarter. In his *Divine Legation* you are always entertained. He carries you round and round, without carrying you forward to the point, but then you have no wish to be carried forward." [2] Combining a severe and strict orthodoxy of opinion with a conspicuous laxity in his personal conduct, he was culpably negligent in his spiritual duties and most overbearing and abusive to those who ventured to disagree with his views. As an illustration of his intemperate language and want of self-control, he declared in the House of Lords, of the notorious Wilkes, "that the blackest fiends in hell will not keep company with him when he arrives there." [3] His theology, in common with the prevalent ideas of the eighteenth century, was based entirely on reason, and thus he was bitterly opposed to all forms of "enthusiasm," and "had a profound contempt for the Methodists, pronouncing Whitefield a madman and Wesley little better." [4]

[1] Hurd's *Life of Warburton*, vol. i. p. 84 (1794).
[2] Chambers, *Book of Days*, vol. i. p. 745 (1888).
[3] Ibid.
[4] Stoughton, *Religion in England under Anne and the Georges*, vol. ii. p. 11.

Richard Hurd, Bishop of Lichfield 1775, and Worcester 1781–1808, Warburton's great friend, was a man of a very different character. A careful and correct scholar, reserved and dignified in manner, so much so that George III. pronounced him "the most naturally polite man he had ever known." [1] Very fond of elaborate and costly state, he was a personal and trusted friend of the King, who appointed him tutor to his two eldest sons. Pious, but exceedingly conventional in his religion, he frequently preached against the Methodists, and could see nothing but fanatical insanity in the great Evangelical revival which was then at its height. Probably the most active and zealous prelate of this period was Beilby Porteus, who was Bishop of London 1787–1808. Intent on reforming the prevalent Church abuses, he was a keen sympathiser with the Evangelical movement, an advocate of the Sunday-school system, and a warm supporter of Wilberforce in his Anti-Slave Trade crusade. He did his utmost to promote a better regard for Sunday, and also revived the observance of Lent, which had been long neglected in his diocese. Mention also must be made of Shute Barrington, Bishop of Durham, the friend of Hannah More and Wilberforce, who throughout his long life (1734–1826) actively sympathised with all good work; while in Bishop Horsley, who was successively Bishop of St. Davids, Rochester, and St. Asaph, the Church found a defender of the Catholic faith, if not equally as able, at least more vehement than his famous predecessor, Daniel Waterland.

The name of George Horne, Bishop of Norwich 1789-92, deserves special notice on account of his intimate connection with a school of theologians who were commonly styled "Hutchinsonians," because they largely adopted the opinions of John Hutchinson, a clergyman who died in 1737. Hutchinson had written a book, called *Moses Principia*, in opposition to the philosophy of Isaac Newton, but it was his intense veneration for Holy Scripture, and his mystical and spiritual interpretation of it, which attracted Horne and the later "Hutchinsonians," for they were strongly opposed to the merely intellectual discussion and criticism of Divine truth which was then so prevalent. Horne was an earnest and popular preacher, of sincere piety and winning manners. He also strongly resented the invidious use of opprobrious nicknames. "If," he says, "a man preaches Christ that He is the end of the law and the fulness of the Gospel,

[1] Kilvert's *Life of Hurd*, p. 199 (1860).

'You need not mind him; he is a Hutchinsonian.' If he mentions the assistance and direction of the Holy Spirit, with the necessity of prayer, mortification, and the taking up the cross, 'O, he is a Methodist.' If he talks of the divine right of episcopacy, with a word concerning the danger of schism, 'Just going over to Popery.'"[1]

Prominent among the Hutchinsonians was Bishop Horne's great friend, William Jones, perpetual curate of Nayland, whose writings, especially his *Catholic Doctrine of the Trinity*, were most valuable treatises in the cause of orthodoxy.

CHAPTER VI

THE REVIVAL MOVEMENT

ALTHOUGH it is impossible to explain fully the causes which led to such a fearful spread of impiety and irreligion during the eighteenth century, yet there are some circumstances which in a measure contributed to it. The silencing of Convocation, owing to the unfortunate "Bangorian Controversy," had had a disastrous effect on the healthy life and action of the Church, and the want of a unanimous official declaration on disputed doctrinal questions, or of a united effort to restrain prevalent abuses, seriously curtailed its influence and authority. The schism caused by the Nonjurors had also resulted in the withdrawal from the ranks of the clergy of a large number of the more spiritually-minded High Churchmen, while the usefulness of those who remained within the Establishment was largely impaired by their known Jacobite and Tory sympathies. The extent to which the clergy of the earlier part of the century were permeated with this political spirit is shown from a statement of the Nonjuror Bishop Hickes, who "thanked God that the main body of the clergy were in their hearts Jacobites."[2]

But probably the prevalent theology of the day accounted more than anything else for the degeneracy of the times. The Low Church party and the bulk of the influential clergy were permeated with Latitudinarian teaching, and too often there was

[1] Bishop Horne's Works, iv. pp. 166–7 (1818).
[2] *Essays and Reviews*, p. 309 (1860).

D

but a thin line between this and Deistic opinions. The rationalistic spirit had captivated almost all minds. Religious zeal or "enthusiasm" was a term of scorn and reproach, not only because of its associations with the extravagant and sometimes heretical opinions of the Anabaptists, "Fifth Monarchists," or Quakers of the previous century, but also because any doctrine of divine spiritual enlightenment was entirely out of harmony with the attempt to exclude from religion everything outside the boundary of "reason" and the human understanding. "The entire sympathies of a host of eminent divines of the eighteenth century were with the reasonable rather than with the spiritual side of religion."[1] The direct personal work of the Holy Spirit on the hearts and lives of men was regarded by general consent to have been limited to apostolic and early Christian times, and therefore not to be expected in later ages.

Thus the sermons and theological teaching of the day were largely mere moral essays, with little or no attempt to bring home conviction of sin to the conscience, but rather appealing to the inherent reasonableness of virtue and godliness than pointing to the only source of power which could enable men to attain them. "The obligation of obedience, the appeal to our desire of our own welfare, was the substance of the practical teaching of the age."[2] The celebrated lawyer Sir W. Blackstone, who about the middle of the century went to hear every clergyman of note in London, stated that "he did not hear a single discourse having more Christianity in it than the writings of Cicero, and that it would have been impossible for him to discover from what he heard whether the preacher were a follower of Confucius, of Mahomet, or of Christ."[3] Even if this description be somewhat exaggerated, there is no doubt that the instructions of the clergy had little or no effect in stemming the moral degradation of the times.

It is scarcely possible in the present day to realise the fearful extent to which godlessness and vice had been carried by the middle of the eighteenth century, and were it not for the numerous reliable contemporary testimonies it would be difficult to credit the deplorable state of society which then existed. Even as early as 1709 a contemporary authority had asserted that "the doctrine and discipline of our Church is exploded, and our holy religion become a name which is almost everywhere spoken

[1] *Eng. Ch. in 18th Cent.*, p. 237. [2] *Essays and Reviews*, p. 325.
[3] Ryle, *Christian Leaders*, p. 15.

against."[1] In 1753 Sir J. Barnard declared that "at present it really seems to be the fashion for a man to declare himself of no religion,"[2] while Bishop Butler's well-known pessimistic description of the state of religion has become almost classical. "It is come," he said, "I know not how, to be taken for granted by many persons that Christianity is not so much as a subject of inquiry, but that it is now at length discovered to be fictitious. Accordingly they treat it as if in the present age this were an agreed-on point among all people of discernment, and nothing remained but to set it up as a principal subject of mirth and ridicule, as it were by way of reprisals for its having so long interrupted the pleasures of the world."[3]

A disgracefully low standard of public opinion prevailed on all moral questions and affected all classes of society. Vice and profanity were as open and shameless at the Court as in the cottage. "Of the prominent statesmen of the time the greater part were unbelievers in any form of Christianity, and distinguished for the grossness and immorality of their lives. . . . Purity and fidelity to the marriage vow were sneered out of fashion, and Lord Chesterfield instructed his son in the art of seduction as part of a polite education."[4] Horace Walpole wrote in 1751 that "the vices of the lower people were increased to a degree of robbery and murder beyond example."[5] Drunkenness was fearfully common, and considered no disgrace; men were known from the number of bottles of port they could drink at a sitting! It is related that Sir Robert Walpole's father took the precaution of first making his young son intoxicated in order that he might not witness his own father in that condition, while a common street sign ran, "Drunk for 1d., dead drunk for 2d., clean straw for nothing."

The stage ever since the days of the Restoration had been notoriously licentious, while even the best literature was tainted with impurity. Sir Walter Scott, who lived only a generation later, stated that "the writings of even the most esteemed poets (of this time) contained passages which would now be accounted to deserve the pillory, nor was the tone of conversation more pure than that of composition."[6]

[1] Bishop Beveridge's *Private Thoughts*, Preface (1709).
[2] *Parl. Hist.*, vol. xiv. p. 1389 (1813).
[3] Advertisement to *Analogy*.
[4] Green, *Short Hist. of Eng. People*, p. 717 (1885).
[5] *Memoirs*, Reign of George II., vol. i. p. 38 (1822).
[6] Andrews, *The Eighteenth Century*, p. 328 (1856).

Amusements and pastimes were brutal and degrading; prize-fighting, even among women,[1] was common, and bull-baiting and cock-fighting furnished the Sunday afternoon's entertainment in most villages, while the very frequent public executions were diversions as popular and fashionable as the Lord Mayor's Show. The barbarous practice of burning instead of hanging women actually survived till 1789. Violence and crime were rather fostered than restrained by a most iniquitous criminal code, which enacted capital punishment for no less than two hundred and fifty-three offences. It is easy to see the wit which must have prompted the old adage, "One may as well be hanged for a sheep as a lamb," when we learn that a pickpocket was liable to the death penalty as well as the murderer.[2]

It is not difficult, from this brief survey of the state of society, to form some idea of the tremendous need which must have existed for a revival of true spiritual religion at the time when the great religious movement of the century which was destined to exercise such far-reaching influence on the English Church was started under Wesley and Whitefield. But before noticing the origin of the Methodists revival it is well to bear in mind that the great intellectual controversies with Arians, Deists, and sceptics, which had been waged with such conspicuous ability by eminent theologians during the first half of the century, had done much to prepare the ground for the stirring appeals of the later evangelists, whose earnest messages went straight to the heart and conscience, and dealt not merely with a correct theoretical belief, but with its practical effect on life and conduct.

A special feature of the great spiritual revival of the latter half of the century, and one which differentiated it from any modern "mission," was its spontaneous growth. Although it owed an incalculable debt to the enthusiasm of its great leaders, yet it by no means depended on the marvellous evangelistic efforts of Wesley or Whitefield. A deep spiritual awakening sprang up almost simultaneously in different districts, and in places where the names of the great revivalists were not even known. The foundations of the Methodist movement date back to the year

[1] A record of June 22, 1768, stated: "Wednesday last two women fought for a new chemise valued at half a guinea, in Spafields near Islington. The battle was won by the woman called 'Bruising Peg,' who beat her antagonist in a terrible manner." Andrews, *The Eighteenth Century*, p. 58.)

[2] In 1735 there is a record of an execution "for stealing two pieces of sarcenet out of a shop." (Ibid., p. 280.)

1729, when a small company of "serious" Oxford men began to meet together to study the Greek Testament. These little gatherings had been started by Charles Wesley, a student of Christ Church, but his elder brother John, who was Fellow of Lincoln College, soon joined them and became their recognised leader. They only numbered four at first, but they soon increased to about twenty-seven members, and in 1733 they obtained a powerful recruit in George Whitefield, a poor servitor of Pembroke College.

At first the main object of this select company was to govern their daily lives by fixed rules of conduct and to fill up every moment of their time with some definite and useful work. It was, in fact, a little society modelled on the same lines as the "Religious Societies" of young men which had been started at the close of the previous century, and had spread so rapidly that in 1710 there were forty-two in London and Westminster alone. The ecclesiastical views of this little Oxford band of reformers were distinctly "high." They scrupulously observed the appointed fasts and festivals of the Church, and lived such severely ascetic lives that they ran the risk of seriously endangering their health. Morgan, one of the original four, who died young, was supposed to have hastened his death by the austerities he practised. They also believed in praying for the faithful departed, and excited much opposition amongst the careless undergraduates of their day by their weekly participation of the Communion. They were "all of one judgment and one heart, and all tenacious of order to the last degree and observant for conscience' sake of every rule of the Church."[1] Their sober and pious conduct attracted attention, and they were soon held up to universal ridicule and styled in derision the "Holy Club," and later on "Methodists," in allusion to their regular habits of life. Samuel Wesley, the High Church rector of Epworth, wrote: "I hear my son John has the honour of being styled the Father of the Holy Club; if it be so, I am sure I must be the grandfather of it."[2] They soon turned their attention to practical Christian work, and obtained the permission of the Bishop of Oxford to visit the sick poor and the condemned prisoners in Oxford Castle, where, as in all gaols at this time, criminals of all degrees and of both sexes were herded together in foul and loathsome dungeons unfit for cattle.

[1] Tyerman's *Life of Wesley*, i. 69 (1870).
[2] Southey's *Life of Wesley*, p. 40.

These early Methodists were greatly influenced by two books, just published, by William Law, the famous Nonjuring mystic; and John Wesley was much encouraged by the spiritual help and counsel he received from the author of the *Serious Call* and *Christian Perfection*. "Religion," said Law to Wesley, "is the most plain, simple thing in the world. It is only 'We love Him because He first loved us.'"[1]

In 1735 the little Oxford society was scattered, as its leader accepted the post of S.P.G. missionary to the settlers and Indians in the newly formed colony of Georgia; but we must reserve for another chapter the later history of Methodism and the fuller consideration of the character and work of the man who was pre-eminently its leader and founder.

CHAPTER VII

JOHN WESLEY AND THE GROWTH OF METHODISM

JOHN WESLEY was born at Epworth in 1703. At the age of six he had an almost miraculous escape from being burnt alive, as his father's rectory had been set on fire by some miscreants, and John, who had been overlooked in the confusion, was only just snatched from the bedroom before the burning roof fell in. This providential deliverance was strongly impressed on his mind, and in after life he used to speak of himself as in a double sense "a brand plucked out of the burning." It also led his mother to take especial care in the training of this child whom she had so nearly lost. Wesley owed much to the wise and patient home training he received; his mother's practical piety and sound advice were especially valuable in moulding his character and fitting him for his after life. Thus, at the close of his undergraduate days, his mother, seeking to overcome his scruples against taking holy orders, wrote: "In good earnest resolve to make religion the business of your life: for, after all, that is the one thing that, strictly speaking, is necessary; all things beside are comparatively little to the purposes of life. I heartily wish you would now enter upon a strict examination of yourself, that you may know whether you have a reasonable hope of salvation by Jesus Christ. If you have the satisfaction of knowing, it will

[1] Southey (*ante*), p. 48.

abundantly reward your pains; if you have not, you will find a more reasonable occasion for tears than can be met with in a tragedy." [1]

On another occasion, when exercised over the question of pleasure and recreation, his mother wrote: "Would you judge of the lawfulness or unlawfulness of pleasure, take this rule:—whatever weakens your reason, impairs the tenderness of your conscience, obscures your sense of God, or takes off the relish of spiritual things; in short, whatever increases the strength and authority of your body over your mind, that thing is sin to you, however innocent it may be in itself." [1]

Wesley was educated at the Charterhouse and Christ Church, Oxford. His scruples concerning ordination were removed largely by reading Jeremy Taylor's *Rules of Holy Living and Dying*, and in 1725 he was ordained by Bishop Potter of Oxford, and in the following year elected to a Fellowship at Lincoln College. Shortly afterwards he acted as curate to his father, taking charge of an outlying parish at Wroote; but he only remained there two years, and returned to Oxford in time to take the lead of the little society of "Methodists" which his brother Charles had just started.

The mission to Georgia which, after much hesitation, he undertook in 1735, in company with his brother Charles and Benjamin Ingham, one of the earlier members of the Oxford society, only lasted about two years and was a distinct failure. His rigid adherence to an exclusive and exacting Church discipline was entirely out of harmony with the freer spirit of colonial life. He incurred the open hostility of his flock by insisting on baptising all children by immersion, and by refusing to read the burial service over a Dissenter, or to administer the Communion to an earnest Christian who was not a member of the church of England, unless he consented to be re-baptised. He embroiled himself in an unfortunate love affair, and at length was forced to return to England because of an action brought against him by the lady in question for injudiciously and uncharitably repelling her from the Communion Table.

Wesley seems to have been peculiarly unwise and unfortunate in his matrimonial ventures. Some years later he married a widow named Vizeille, who proved to be in every way an unsuitable companion in life. Besides not being in full sympathy with his work, she possessed a violent temper, and was so out-

[1] Southey (*ante*), p. 25.

rageously jealous that she must have rendered his life almost unbearable. She opened and even confiscated his letters and papers, and went so far as to show his correspondence to his enemies with the intention of damaging his reputation. She constantly left him, returning only after his earnest entreaties, and at length disappeared with part of his *Journals*, stating that she never intended to return. Wesley merely records in his *Journal* the somewhat humorous comment: "I did not forsake her, I did not dismiss her, I will not recall her." [1]

His visit to America had, however, one very important result in bringing him into touch with the Moravian Brethren, and his intercourse with them led him to doubt seriously his own spiritual condition. One of their number asked him, "Do you know Jesus Christ?" "I know he is the Saviour of the world," Wesley replied. "True," rejoined the Moravian, "but do you know He has saved *you*?" Wesley answered: "I hope He has died to save me." This close questioning evidently led to anxious self-examination, as on his return to England he solemnly confesses: "It is now two years and almost four months since I left my native country in order to teach the Georgian Indians the nature of Christianity. But what have I learnt myself meantime? Why—what I the least of all suspected: —that I who went to America to convert others was never myself converted to God." [2] In this unsettled state of mind he met Peter Boehler, a Moravian missionary on his way to Georgia, and was astounded at the joy and holiness which he affirmed were the natural results of a real living faith in Christ. "In the hands of God," said Wesley, "I was clearly convinced of unbelief, of the want of that faith whereby alone we are saved." [3] He also failed altogether to comprehend the possibility of a "sudden conversion," a doctrine which was certainly little in harmony with the spirit of eighteenth century theology. He could not understand "how this faith could be given in a moment, how a man could at once be thus turned from darkness to light, from sin and misery to righteousness and joy in the Holy Ghost." A closer study of the Greek Testament, however, led him to give an intellectual assent to Boehler's teaching, "as to his utter

[1] *Journal*, Jan. 23, 1771.
[2] Wesley afterwards confessed that "he had even then the faith of a servant, though not that of a son." (Ibid., Feb. 7, 1736, and Jan. 29, 1738.)
[3] Southey, p. 114.

astonishment he found scarce any instances there of other than instantaneous conversions";[1] but it was not till the memorable evening of the 24th May 1738, when he attended a little religious gathering in Aldersgate Street, that he realised by personal experience his own definite spiritual awakening. As some one was reading Luther's Preface to the Epistle to the Romans, Wesley records, "I felt my heart strangely warmed, I felt I did trust in Christ, Christ alone for salvation, and an assurance was given me that He had taken away *my* sins, even *mine*, and saved me from the law of sin and death."[2]

His brother Charles had passed through a similar experience a few days previously, and these very real spiritual crises produced a marked effect on their future teaching. The doctrine of the "New Birth," explained as a sudden conscious spiritual change, producing a full assurance of present salvation, was continually enforced as the *necessary* experience for every true Christian. Their youthful enthusiasm and undoubted earnestness for the salvation of souls at first obscured their calmer judgment, and they failed to recognise that it is impossible to limit the regenerating work of the Holy Spirit to any particular time or method. In later years this mistake was acknowledged, and Wesley declared: "When fifty years ago my brother Charles and I, in the simplicity of our hearts, told the good people of England that unless they *knew* their sins were forgiven they were under the wrath and curse of God, I marvel they did not stone us! The Methodists, I hope, know better now. We preach assurance, as we always did, as a common privilege of the children of God; but we do not enforce it under pain of damnation, denounced on all who enjoy it not."[3]

The cardinal doctrine of Justification by Faith, so strongly emphasised in Article XI., was from this time forward the foundation of all Methodist teaching. "Believing," Wesley rightly explained, "was the act of man, but it was the gift of God," and a true faith "was a sure trust and confidence which a man hath in God, that, through the merits of Christ, his sins are forgiven and he reconciled to the favour of God."[4]

In noticing the various phases and changes in the marvellous career of this great evangelist, it is important to remember the supremely disinterested purpose and motive that guided his

[1] *Journal*, April 21, 1738. [2] Ibid., May 24, 1738.
[3] Southey, p. 175.
[4] *Ch. of Eng. Homily of Salvation* (*Journal*, April 21, 1738).

every action. Wesley's ruling passion in life was to save souls, to promote the love of God in the hearts and lives of his fellow-men; everything was subordinated to this one grand aim: his own distinct ecclesiastical views, his devotion to the Church, his obedience to its authority and discipline, all had to be either sacrificed or modified if they conflicted with, or hindered, this one supreme object. It was this singleness of purpose that led him to disregard the parochial system of the Church. "If there be a law," he wrote in 1761, "that a minister of Christ who is not suffered to preach the Gospel in church should not preach it elsewhere . . . I judge that law to be absolutely sinful and that it is sinful to obey it." [1] And in justifying his conduct to a friend who challenged the consistency of his action on Catholic principles, he wrote: "If by Catholic principles you mean any other than Scriptural, they weigh nothing with me; I allow no other rule, whether of faith or practice, than the Holy Scriptures. But on Scriptural grounds I do not think it hard to justify whatever I do. God in Scripture commands me, according to my power, to instruct the ignorant, reform the wicked, and confirm the virtuous; man forbids me to do this in another man's parish, that is, in effect, to do it at all, seeing I have no parish of my own. Whom then shall I hear, God or man? I look upon all the world as my parish, thus far, I mean, that in whatever part of it I am I judge it meet, right, and my bounden duty, to declare unto all that are willing to hear the glad tidings of salvation." [2] He retained, however, to a large extent throughout his life his distinct preference for High Church views and usages. Every Friday was scrupulously set apart as a day of abstinence, and was enjoined as such in his school at Kingswood, and he insisted on the men and women sitting separately in his chapels. "He was," as an intimate friend described him, "a Church of England man of the highest tone . . . even in the more circumstantial parts; there was not a service or a ceremony, a gesture or a habit, for which he had not an unfeigned predilection." [3]

Thus, when George Whitefield, who had commenced the novel practice of field preaching, requested him to take his place during his absence in Georgia, Wesley wrote: "I could scarcely reconcile myself to this strange way of preaching in the fields,

[1] Cf. *Eng. Ch. in 18th Cent.*, p. 324, note 1.
[2] *Journal*, June 11, 1739.
[3] Southey's *Life of Wesley*, vol. ii. p. 319 (1858).

having been all my life, till very lately, so tenacious of every point relating to decency and order, that I should have thought the saving of souls almost a sin if it had not been done in church." [1] Although this practice was then generally condemned as "irregular" or unorthodox, yet as a recent authority [2] well points out, it was neither unlawful nor even irregular "on any true Church principles," and Wesley soon felt himself fully justified in adopting it by the wonderful results which followed. Men and women, often the very outcasts of society, who would never have been persuaded to enter any church, assembled in multitudes to listen to the earnest appeals of the great preacher, and numbers were reclaimed from lives of sin and degradation. A thoroughly impartial authority states that "the doctrines the Methodist teacher taught proved themselves capable of arousing in great masses of men an enthusiasm of piety which was hardly surpassed in the first days of Christianity. . . . Methodism planted a firm and enduring religious sentiment in the midst of the most brutal and neglected portions of the population." [3] Wesley's sermons, although inferior in point of eloquence to those of Whitefield, were exceptionally clear, logical, and popular in style. His main aim was to bring home the guilt of sin to the consciences of his hearers and then point them to the free and present forgiveness of the Saviour, as he fully believed in the present work and power of the Holy Spirit on the human heart, which was not left, as generally taught them, merely to its own reason.

It is singular that, although a distinctly cultured and intellectual man, Wesley had a decided preference for ministering to the lower classes, and never felt that he had any mission to those in the upper ranks of society. "To speak rough truth," he said, "I do not desire any intercourse with any persons of quality, I mean for my own sake. They do me no good, and I fear I can do none to them." [4] There is abundant evidence, however, to prove the marked effect his preaching had on the lives of the humble. On one occasion, after he had been itinerating in a country village, some of his hearers had become such changed characters that their neighbours, in alarm, brought them before the magistrate. When he inquired as to the nature of their offence, "Plaise, your worship," said one of the accusers, "they

[1] *Journal*, March 29, 1739. [2] Overton and Relton (*ante*), p. 92.
[3] Lecky, *Hist. of Eng. in 18th Cent.*, ii. p. 600 (1878).
[4] Southey, p. 219.

pretend to be better than other people, and pray from morning till night." "Have they done nothing else?" "Yes, sir," said an old man, "an't plaise your worship, they have convarted my wife; till she went among them she had a tongue! but now she is as quiet as a lamb!" "Carry them back," said the magistrate, "and let them convert all the scolds in the town."[1]

When we remember the difficulty and fatigue of travelling a hundred and fifty years ago, we are amazed at the record of Wesley's itinerating labours. Even in his eightieth year he states that he still travelled four thousand to five thousand miles a year, and during his evangelistic tours he is said to have preached altogether forty thousand sermons. It is not surprising that this fervent religious zeal and activity should have met with great antagonism from the bulk of the clergy of that time, who seemed so largely indifferent to the spiritual stagnation which prevailed. The Methodists were denied the use of parish pulpits, often, it is feared, through jealousy of the large congregations they attracted, and were loudly denounced on all sides. Many of the bishops openly condemned them. Bishop Lavington compared them with the "Papists," and declared that they were "a dangerous and presumptuous sect, animated with an enthusiastical and fanatical spirit." Their doctrines and methods were regarded as unorthodox by High Churchmen, and were equally obnoxious to the Latitudinarian principles of the Low Churchmen, who considered all appeals to the emotional side of man's nature as "unreasonable" enthusiasm, or dangerous mysticism.

To the antagonism of the clergy was often added, in the early years of the movement, the opposition and persecution of a prejudiced or ignorant populace. Methodist preachers were frequently mobbed and ill-treated, "some received serious injury, others were held under water till they were nearly dead, and of the women who attended them, some were so treated by the cowardly and brutal populace that they never thoroughly recovered."[2] When we remember the religious spirit of the century we are forced to admit that no better treatment from either clergy or laity could have been expected, but nevertheless we cannot but deplore the hostile and unsympathetic attitude very largely adopted by the hierarchy. Although there were tendencies from the first in the Methodist movement which eventually led to its final separation from the Church, yet under a wise and sympathetic official guidance or supervision these might have been

[1] Andrews, *Life of Whitefield*, p. 160. [2] Southey, p. 214.

counteracted, and the full results of this great revival might have been retained, and would certainly have proved an incalculable blessing to the Anglican Church. It is nearly certain that had the "Church Army" arisen in the eighteenth century, it would have been equally ostracised by the clergy, and its evangelistic methods condemned as unorthodox and unlawful.

It is well here to notice the stages and causes which gradually led to the complete alienation of Methodism from the National Church. Its separation was certainly the result of circumstances rather than of design, as there is ample evidence to prove the strong and permanent attachment of its great leader to Church principles. John Wesley, whatever his definite actions may seem to indicate, had never any intention or desire for his followers to leave the Church of England. "In every possible way," he wrote in 1783, "I have advised the Methodists to keep to the Church ... if ever the Methodists in general were to leave the church, I must leave them."[1] Both he and his brother Charles frequently exhorted their followers never to think of separating from the Established Church. "Ye yourselves," said Wesley, "were at first called in the Church of England, and though ye have and will have a thousand temptations to leave it, and set up for yourselves, regard them not. Be Church of England men still." He persistently refused to allow the Methodists to hold their Sunday services in Church hours, as it seemed to signify "a formal separation from the Church." "I never," he says in 1790, "had any design of separating from the Church, I have no such design now, I do not believe the Methodists in general design it. I do and will do all that is in my power to prevent such an event. . . . I declare once more that I live and die a member of the Church of England, and that none who regard my judgment or advice will ever separate from it."[2]

Certainly the bitter antagonism displayed by the clergy to the movement had no small share in bringing about the final alienation from the Church, but a far more direct cause than this was the attitude of the lay preachers. The small number of ordained clergy who actively supported him had obliged Wesley to employ laymen as preachers to the increasing number of adherents. These men soon felt their position to be irksome and anomalous. They had neither the status of Dissenting ministers nor the privileges of a Church clergyman, as they were strictly forbidden

[1] Tyerman, *Life of Wesley*, iii. 391.
[2] Southey, Appendix, pp. 366–9.

to administer the Sacraments. Their ambition, therefore, constantly provoked a spirit of jealousy of their clerical superiors, and a secret hatred of that ecclesiastical discipline which so materially curtailed their office and authority. Charles Wesley, who frequently came into collision with them, wrote to his brother: "I am sorry you yielded to the lay preachers. I think them in the greatest danger through pride. . . . The preachers do not love the Church of England. What must be the consequence when we are gone? A separation is inevitable." [1] Another unavoidable cause of schism was the legal position of the Methodist meeting-houses. Owing to a peculiar effect of the Conventicle Act, the preachers discovered that in order to save themselves from arrest they were obliged to be licensed as Dissenting teachers. Wesley strove against this as long as he could. "Let all our preachers," he urged, "go to church. Let all our people go constantly. Receive the Sacrament at every opportunity. Warn them against calling our Society *a church*, or our preachers *ministers*, our houses *meeting-houses*, call them plain preaching houses. Do not license them as such." [2] Nevertheless, from 1760 their chapels began to be licensed, and this step led to the withdrawal of the support of several of the Evangelical clergy. Grimshaw of Haworth severed his connection at once, writing to Charles Wesley that "the Methodists are no longer members of the Church of England. They are as real a body of Dissenters from her as the Presbyterians, Baptists, Quakers, or any body of Independents. . . . I hereby assure you that I disclaim all further and future connection with them." [3]

But the act that finally crossed the Rubicon was Wesley's assumption of the power of ordination. Relying on the interchangeableness of the offices of bishop and presbyter [4] in the primitive Church, in 1784 he assumed the right to set apart Dr. Coke, an English clergyman who since 1776 had acted as his chief lieutenant, as "superintendent" of the Methodists in America. The situation was exceedingly difficult. The Colonial Church had long been in need of a bishop, and the large number of Methodists who had been converted through the labours of Whitefield made this need all the more urgent. Owing to the action of the English Government, the Anglican bishops had been so far powerless to supply this want, and the War of Independence had rendered their position still more difficult. Under these

[1] Southey, p. 332.
[2] Tyerman's *Wesley*, ii. 385.
[3] Ibid., p. 268.
[4] Cf. *Journal*, Jan. 20, 1746.

circumstances Wesley considered himself justified in intervening. Coke soon changed his title to that of bishop, and together with Francis Asbury, whom he had set apart as his co-adjutor, ordained others to minister to the American Methodists. Not content with this, Wesley proceeded further and in 1785 ordained lay-leaders to minister in Scotland, and a few years later set apart others to officiate in England.

In spite, however, of his brother's regrets and remonstrances, Wesley steadily refused to recognise the inevitable consequence of these definite acts. Charles Wesley wrote at the time to a brother clergyman: "Lord Mansfield told me last year that ordination was separation. This my brother does not and will not see, and that he has renounced the principles and practices of his whole life."[1] Wesley, on the other hand, maintained that the Church of England was not concerned in acts performed for America or Scotland. "Whatever is done in America and Scotland," he wrote in 1786, "is no separation from the Church of England. I have no thought of this."[2]

A prominent feature of the Methodist movement, and one which contributed in no small degree to its rapid growth, was the wonderful organisation, which the conspicuous genius of Wesley built up step by step as the need for it arose. A difficulty having arisen over the payment of a debt on the first meeting-house, which had been built at Bristol in 1739, it was arranged to divide the Society into small classes with a leader for each, who should call on the other members each week for his contribution to the expenses. Thus on somewhat similar lines to the earlier Religious Societies, arose the "Class Meetings," which soon exercised a most thorough discipline over the members of each Society as it was formed. "It can scarcely be conceived" says Wesley, "what advantages have been reaped from this little prudential regulation. Many now happily experienced that Christian fellowship of which they had not so much as an idea before. They began to bear one another's burdens and to care for each other. . . . Evil men were detected and reproved . . . if they obstinately persisted in their sins it was openly declared they were not of us."[3]

The "Conference" soon followed on the Class. The first was held in 1744, when Wesley invited "the several clergymen and all who served him as sons in the Gospel to meet him in

[1] Smith's *Hist. of Methodism*, i. 517.

[2] *Dict. Nat. Biog.*, vol. lx. p. 211. [3] Southey, p. 193.

London, and to give him advice concerning the best method of carrying on the work of God." [1] The formation of definite "Circuits," to which lay Itinerants and Local Preachers were appointed by the Conference, completed the system. The power of administering this elaborate organisation was vested in Wesley, whose authority and supremacy over all the Methodist Societies was practically absolute, and descended to such minute details as the particular construction of the chapel pews and windows. He laid down very full and stringent rules of conduct for the guidance of his lay helpers. Even the chapels were not allowed to be vested in trustees, but in "Wesley and the Conference," and he alone possessed the power of appointing the preachers. In 1784, realising the necessity of legally securing the chapel property after his death, Wesley somewhat arbitrarily selected in his "Deed of Declaration" one hundred members of the Conference to hold the estates of the Connection and to nominate the preachers for the chapels and circuits. Wesley's supreme authority was, however, cheerfully acquiesced in by his followers. "No founder of a monastic order ever more entirely possessed the respect, as well as the love and admiration, of his disciples." [2]

If the formation and development of Methodism were chiefly due to its open-air preaching and splendid organisation, certainly the maintenance of the life and enthusiasm of the Societies was largely owing to its hymnology. The Wesleys possessed a gift for poetry, but it was Charles Wesley (1708–88) who specially excelled in this direction. He is said to have composed nearly seven thousand hymns, many of which still hold a foremost place in modern collections, and voice the needs and aspirations of Christians of almost all persuasions. We can well understand the strength and inspiration which these early Methodist converts must have received in times of difficulty and persecution, as they joined in such stirring hymns as "Ye servants of God, your Master proclaim," "Oh, for a heart to praise my God," "Lo! He comes, with clouds descending," "Oh, for a thousand tongues to sing," and "Soldiers of Christ! arise."

Wesley's long life gave him a unique opportunity of witnessing the truly wonderful progress of the organisation he had founded, and which in its earlier years met with such bitter opposition. At his death in 1791 the number of Methodist preachers in Great Britain and America amounted to 511, while the members in

[1] Smith's *Hist. of Methodism,* i. 210. [2] Southey, p. 222.

connection with the various Societies had risen to nearly one hundred and thirty-five thousand. As long as he lived he had prevented any formal or open breach between his followers and the Church of England, but as soon as his powerful influence was removed the antipathy to the Church felt by a large number of the Methodists could no longer be restrained. Wesley had always strongly opposed the administration of the Communion in his own chapels, and frequently urged his converts to communicate at their parish churches. This rule had been very generally observed, but in 1795 the final link which bound the Methodists to the Church was severed when the Conference officially sanctioned the administration of the Lord's Supper in chapels where the majority of members desired it. From this time forward Methodism existed as a distinct and separate organisation.

CHAPTER VIII

GEORGE WHITEFIELD AND THE CALVINISTIC CONTROVERSY

It is time now to consider the life and character of the one who was pre-eminently the preacher of the Methodist revival. If Charles Wesley excelled as the singer, and John was conspicuous as the organiser, Whitefield was undoubtedly the orator of the movement. He possessed an insatiable passion for preaching. "Oh," he said, "that I could fly from pole to pole preaching the everlasting Gospel." [1] A recent Church historian has well said that "he went forth into the world filled with the one burning desire of doing good to his fellow-men and of extending the kingdom of his Divine Master." [2] Certainly his whole life was an almost literal fulfilment of his ideal definition of a true faith. "A true faith in Christ Jesus," said Whitefield, "will not suffer us to be *idle*. No; it is an active, lively, restless principle; it fills the heart so that it cannot be easy till it is doing something for Jesus Christ." [3] The record of his prodigious labours seems

[1] Andrews, *Life of Whitefield*, p. 256.
[2] Overton, *Eng. Ch. in 18th Cent.*, p. 377.
[3] Andrews, *Life of Whitefield*, p. 70.

almost incredible. Besides his enormous correspondence, he is supposed to have spoken publicly on an average from forty to sixty hours a week, and during the thirty-four years of his ministerial work to have preached no less than eighteen thousand times. In those days of slow and difficult travelling he was in Ireland twice and in Scotland fifteen times, while he itinerated in almost every corner of England and Wales. He paid seven visits to America, travelling hundreds of miles on his mission campaigns while there. "The truth is," said Henry Venn, in preaching his funeral sermon, "that in point of labour this extraordinary servant of God did as much in a few weeks as most of those who exert themselves are able to do in the space of a year." [1]

His early career bears a marked contrast to that of Wesley. Instead of the opportunities for culture and refinement and thorough education afforded by the home training in a country rectory, and the discipline and advantages of a public school life, Whitefield was handicapped by the somewhat degrading associations of the public-house in which he was born and where for a time he was compelled to serve as potboy. He picked up what education he could during an irregular attendance at the local Grammar School. Although his ancestors were either clergymen or people of property and respectability, his father had started in business as a wine merchant and publican at Gloucester. He died when George was only two years old, and the business of the "Bell Inn" proved a failure. Thus it was only through the interest of friends obtaining for George the menial position of servitor at Pembroke College that his mother was able to send him to Oxford in 1732. After he had been there about a year he became acquainted with Charles Wesley, who lent him a book called *The Life of God in the Soul of Man.* "I never knew," says Whitefield, "what true religion was till God sent me that excellent treatise. God soon showed me that true religion was union with God and Christ formed within us. Not till then did I know that I must be a new creature. Like the woman of Samaria, I wrote letters to my relations telling them there was such a thing as the *new birth*; they thought I was going beside myself." [2] He now began "to live by rule that not a moment of time should be lost," and therefore actively associated himself with the little band of Oxford "Methodists." The peace

[1] Gillies, *Life of Whitefield,* p. 330 (1772).
[2] Tyerman's *Life of Whitefield,* vol. i. p. 17 (1890).

and assurance which at first followed upon his conversion were, however, soon succeeded by a "horrible fearfulness and dread" which overwhelmed his soul. This terrible state of spiritual despondency he endeavoured to counteract by a life of the greatest asceticism and by severe mortification of the flesh. Whole days and weeks he spent lying prostrate on the ground, begging for freedom from "those proud hellish thoughts that used to crowd in upon and distract my soul." He fasted twice a week, chose the worst food and wore the meanest apparel, "he kept Lent so strictly that except on Saturdays and Sundays his only food was coarse bread and sage tea without sugar." [1] He resolutely persisted in these voluntary acts of self-denial because, as he tells us, "he thought he found in them great promoters of spiritual life." [2]

A conversation with John Wesley at this time convinced him of the dangerous course he was pursuing, and "at length through his excellent advice he was delivered from those wiles of Satan." The austerities he had practised, however, had so weakened him that he was seriously ill for some time after. His exemplary conduct and self-denying life was soon after brought to the notice of Bishop Benson of Gloucester, who sent for him and made him a present of five guineas, telling him that although he was under the canonical age, "he should think it his duty to ordain him whenever he came for holy orders." [3] Accordingly Whitefield was ordained in 1736 at the age of twenty-two. The solemn service made a profound impression upon him. "Let come what will," he said, "life or death, I shall henceforwards live like one who this day, in the presence of men and angels, took the Holy Sacrament, upon the profession of being inwardly moved by the Holy Ghost to take upon me that ministration in the church. I can call heaven and earth to witness that when the bishop laid his hand upon me I gave myself up to be a martyr for Him who hung upon the cross for me." [4] Even in his first sermon he seems to have made his mark as a preacher of extraordinary power,[5] and his presence in the pulpit soon drew enormous congregations. He acted for a time as curate of Dummer in Hampshire, and although the "poor and illiterate"

[1] Southey, p. 101. [2] R. Philip's *Life of Whitefield*, p. 18 (1838).
[3] Gillies (*ante*), p. 9. [4] Southey, p. 103.
[5] He wrote that "some few mocked . . . and that a complaint had been made to the Bishop that he drove fifteen mad. The worthy prelate wished that the madness might not be forgotten before next Sunday." (Gillies (*ante*), p. 10.)

flock there was little to his taste he faithfully devoted eight hours each day to visiting, catechising, and reading the daily services. Soon after he was invited to London, where he became exceedingly popular and was greatly sought after, especially to preach charity sermons, the collections from his eloquent appeals amounting to over a thousand pounds, a sum far in excess of previous occasions.

At Bristol he preached five times a week, and drew such enormous congregations that "some even hung upon the rails of the organ loft, others climbed upon the leads of the church, and it was only with great difficulty he could get either into the pulpit or reading desk." [1]

He had now been persuaded to succeed Wesley in his work as incumbent of Savannah in Georgia, although large offers of preferment were made to induce him to remain in England.

It is natural to inquire into the reasons for Whitefield's marvellous popularity as a preacher. His personal appearance was entirely in his favour, as he had a fine presence and attractive features, and was remarkable for a natural gracefulness of manner. His voice also was wonderfully powerful and melodious, while his style of preaching was exceedingly popular and persuasive, as he possessed a vivid and almost dramatic power of description. On one occasion, as he was portraying a blind beggar hovering on the brink of a precipice, Lord Chesterfield, the polite but careless sceptic, bounded from his seat, exclaiming, "Good God, he's gone!" [2] Lord Bolingbroke, the famous sceptic, declared, "He is the most extraordinary man in our times. He has the most commanding eloquence I ever heard in any person, his abilities are very considerable, his zeal unquenchable." [3] The celebrated Benjamin Franklin, who listened to one of his sermons on behalf of his much-loved Orphan House in Georgia, stated that at first "I silently resolved he should get nothing from me. I had in my pocket a handful of copper, three or four silver dollars, and five pistoles in gold; as he proceeded I began to soften and concluded to give the copper. Another stroke of his oratory made me ashamed of that and determined me to give the silver, and he finished so admirably that I emptied my pocket wholly into the collector's dish, gold and all." [4]

Whitefield only stayed a few months in Georgia, and returned in 1738 to obtain priest's orders; but he soon discovered that

[1] Gillies (*ante*), p. 13.
[2] *Dict. Nat. Biog.*, vol. lxi. p. 91.
[3] Tyerman's *Whitefield*, vol. ii. p. 194, note 2.
[4] Ibid., vol.i. p. 374.

his strong insistence on the doctrine of the New Birth, coupled with his unheard-of practice of expounding the Scriptures in private houses, gave such offence to the clergy that most of the pulpits were closed to him. In this emergency he commenced preaching in the fields, and soon gathered an earnest congregation from the ignorant and degraded colliers of Kingswood. "Finding," he says, "that the pulpits are denied me, and the poor colliers are ready to perish for lack of knowledge, I went to them and preached on a mount to upwards of two hundred. The first discovery of their being affected was to see the white gutters made by their tears, which plentifully fell down their black cheeks as they came out of their coal pits. Hundreds and hundreds were soon brought under deep convictions, which happily ended in a sound and thorough conversion."[1] Whitefield soon acquired a strong preference for this mode of evangelising. "I always find," he said, "I have most power when I speak in the open air, a proof to me that God is pleased with this way of preaching."[2] From this time, both in England and America, as the parish pulpits became closed to him, Whitefield, in his burning desire "to preach Christ Jesus whether men will hear or whether they will forbear," "took to the fields," or, if invited, used Dissenting chapels. On one occasion, when the Bishop of Bristol requested him to refrain from this latter practice, he replied in justification of his conduct: "My Lord, what can I do? When I acted in the most regular way and was bringing multitudes even of the Dissenters themselves to crowd the churches, without any other reason being given me than that too many followed after me, I was denied the use of them . . . surely your lordship's candour will overlook a little irregularity, since I fear that in these last days wherein we live, we must be obliged to be irregular or, in short, we must do no good at all."[3]

Whitefield's charitable spirit refused to be confined to the limits of one particular church, and he loved Dissenters equally with Churchmen. "I wish," he said, "all names among the saints of God were swallowed up in that one of Christian, I long for professors to leave off placing religion in saying 'I am a churchman,' 'I am a dissenter.' My language to such is, 'Are you of Christ? If so, I love you with all my heart.'"[4]

But this sincere desire for Christian unity in no way interfered with his strong attachment to the Church of England.

[1] Gillies (*ante*), p. 38.
[2] R. Philip (*ante*), p. 130.
[3] Andrews (*ante*), p. 306.
[4] Ibid., p. 78.

He refused resolutely to gratify his friends by forming societies after Wesley's plan, as he hated the very thought of forming a "party." "Those who think I want to make a party or to disturb churches do not know me." [1] "The only Methodism I know," said Whitefield, "is a holy method of dying to ourselves and of living to God." [2] He had a great admiration for the Church Liturgy. "I should rejoice," he preached on one occasion, "to see all the world adhere to her Articles. I am a friend to her Liturgy, and if they did not thrust me out of their churches I would read it every day." [3] He told the Bishop of Bristol, "I shall continue to use her Liturgy wherever a church or chapel is allowed me. . . . Unless thrust out, I shall never leave her, and even then I shall continue to adhere to her doctrines." Before he was fifty his life of incessant toil and overstrain, combined with the constant neglect of his constitution, began to seriously affect him. Unless physically unable, however, he never allowed himself to rest from work. "I had rather wear out than rust out," said Whitefield. "No nestling, no nestling on this side eternity." [4] After 1762 frequent attacks of asthma, his old malady, interrupted his strenuous evangelistic labours, and he found that he was unable, as before, to throw off his sickness by a good "pulpit sweat." When attacked with illness on a previous occasion, he had remarked, "One physician prescribed a perpetual blister, but I have found perpetual preaching a better remedy. When that grand catholicon fails it is over with me." [5]

It was not, however, till 1770 that the body was at length "worn out." He was on a preaching tour in New England, and seemed to have a premonition of his approaching end, as in his last sermon he said: "I go, I go to a rest prepared, my sun has arisen, and by and from heaven has given light to many. 'Tis now about to set—no, it cannot be, but to rise to the zenith of immortal glory. . . . Many shall live when this body is no more, but then—oh, thought divine—I shall be in a world where time, age and sickness, and sorrow are unknown! . . . How willingly would I live for ever to preach Christ! But I die to be with Him." [6] The same night he was seized with a bad attack of asthma, at Newbury Port, and died on 30th September 1770, in the fifty-sixth year of his age.

[1] Tyerman's *Whitefield*, vol. ii. p. 170.
[2] Gillies (*ante*), p. 287.
[3] Tyerman's *Whitefield*, vol. i. p. 298.
[4] Andrews (*ante*), p. 29.
[5] Ibid., p. 304.
[6] Tyerman's *Whitefield*, vol. ii. p. 597.

It is well here to say something of the self-sacrificing work of Selina, Countess of Huntingdon (1707–91), who has been well described as the patroness of the Methodist movement. Through her wide influence the messages of the great evangelists reached a circle of hearers who otherwise would have been practically untouched by the Revival. Regardless of the scorn and ridicule of her own society, she definitely associated herself with the Methodist preachers, and frequently collected in her drawing-room an audience of the most distinguished and fashionable members of the upper classes to listen to their exhortations. She sacrificed her time, position, and wealth to further the cause of the Evangelical revival, and is reputed to have spent as much as £100,000 for this purpose. "Oh, that I may be more and more useful to the souls of my fellow-creatures. I want," she wrote, "to be every moment all life, all zeal, all activity for God, and ever on the stretch for closer communion with Him."[1] Availing herself of her privilege as a peeress of possessing an unlimited number of private chaplains, she appointed a number of the leading Methodist and Evangelical clergy in this capacity, and built chapels adjoining her residences at Brighton, Bath, and Tunbridge Wells, where they could officiate in turn. She was renowned for her hospitality to the clergy who enjoyed her favour. Whitefield wrote in 1750: "Good Lady Huntingdon is a mother in Israel. For a day or two she has had five clergymen under her roof, which makes her ladyship look like a good archbishop with his chaplains around him. Her house is indeed a Bethel. To us in the ministry it looks like a college. We have the Sacrament every morning, heavenly conversation all day, and preach at night. This is to live at Court indeed."[2] Wesley and Whitefield frequently preached to her select congregations, although the latter became her favourite chaplain on account of her strong preference for his Calvinistic opinions. Bishop Benson is said to have regretted that he ordained Whitefield, because he believed that Lady Huntingdon's strong Methodist sympathies, which he tried in vain to overcome, were due to his influence. "My Lord," said the Countess, "mark my words, when you are on your dying bed, that will be one of the few ordinations which you will reflect upon with complacence."[3]

Whitefield's preaching soon made such a wonderful impression

[1] Tyerman, *Wesley's Designated Successor*, p. 151.
[2] Tyerman's *Whitefield*, vol. ii. p. 235.
[3] Tytler, *Countess of Huntingdon and her Circle*, p. 26.

that it became almost a fashion amongst the nobility to visit her chapel at Bath to listen to his eloquence, even bishops being often accommodated in a curtained enclosure known as "Nicodemus's Corner." Through this means the sympathies and valuable services of the Earl of Dartmouth were permanently enlisted in the Evangelical cause, while the Earl of Bath, in 1749 after listening to Whitefield's preaching, sent him a cheque for £50 towards the "Tabernacle," and wrote to Lady Huntingdon that "mocked and reviled as Mr. Whitefield is by all ranks of society, still I contend that the day will come when England will own his greatness as a Reformer, and his goodness as a minister of the most high God." [1]

Even those who strongly disapproved of the Methodist teaching still accepted Lady Huntingdon's invitations. The Duchess of Buckingham wrote: "I thank your ladyship for the information concerning the Methodist preachers; their doctrines are most repulsive and strongly tinctured with impertinence and disrespect towards their superiors in perpetually endeavouring to level all ranks and do away with all distinctions. It is monstrous to be told you have a heart as sinful as the common wretches that crawl on the earth. This is highly offensive and insulting; and I cannot but wonder that your ladyship should relish any sentiments so much at variance with high rank and good breeding. I shall be most happy to accept your kind offer of accompanying me to hear your favourite preacher." [2] George III. was so pleased with her work that he told a prelate who objected to her, "I wish there was a Lady Huntingdon in every diocese in the kingdom." [3]

As the chapels in her "Connexion" multiplied, Lady Huntingdon found it necessary to employ lay preachers, and in order to train these she founded a theological college for students at Trevecca, of which the saintly John Fletcher, Vicar of Madeley, was for some time president. Although the doctrines taught there were expressly declared [4] to be fully in accord with the Church of England, the Liturgy "being regularly and devoutly used," the college can scarcely be regarded as a strictly Church institution, as the rules allowed the students a free choice to enter the ministry of the Church or that of any other Protestant denomination.

[1] *Life and Times of Countess of Huntingdon*, ii. 379 (1844).
[2] *Countess of Huntingdon and her Circle*, p. 47.
[3] *Life and Times of Countess of Huntingdon*, ii. 282. [4] Ibid., ii. 521.

In 1782 the opposition of the incumbent of the parish to clergymen officiating in a chapel in Clerkenwell, recently acquired for Lady Huntingdon, led to the necessity of licensing it as a Dissenting place of worship, and after this, in order to maintain her "Connexion," the Countess was very reluctantly obliged to "secede" from the Church. An "ordination" of two lay preachers in the following year finally completed the breach, and all the Evangelical clergymen hitherto supporting her retired from their positions as her chaplains.

It is sad to have to record the history of the unprofitable "Calvinistic Controversy" which for a time seriously divided the ranks of the Methodist revivalists, and must have grievously harmed their cause. It was to a large extent a revival of the bitter strife between Calvinist and Arminian which had caused such havoc in the Church in the first half of the previous century. It seemed at first likely to alienate permanently the two great leaders of the movement, as the doctrines taught by Wesley approximated to the opinions of the earlier Arminians, while those of Whitefield resembled the teachings of the early Calvinists. It was the old, insoluble problem concerning God's foreknowledge and man's free will, involving the subordinate question of the relationship of faith and works. The extravagant and revolting doctrinal statements and deductions which were being insisted on by some of the more ignorant and fanatical of the Methodists, who held that "a certain number of the people is elected from eternity and these must and shall be saved, and the rest of mankind must and shall be damned," [1] had led Wesley to preach openly against the doctrines of election and final perseverance. This action greatly offended Whitefield, as opposed to his most cherished theological teaching. "Once justified," he states, "is to remain so to all eternity. Here lies the anchor of all my hopes. Our Lord having once loved me He will love me to the end. . . . I now walk by faith ; I work not to keep myself in a justified state but to express my love and gratitude for what Jesus has done for my soul." [2] He therefore wrote to Wesley in 1740 beseeching him not to touch on disputed controversial questions. "For Christ's sake, dear Sir, if possible, never speak *against* election in your sermons ; no one can ever say that I have mentioned it in public discourse, whatever my private sentiments may be. For Christ's sake let us not be divided amongst ourselves." [3]

[1] Wesley's *Journal*, June 19, 1740. [2] Andrews, pp. 122–3. [3] Ibid.

In spite of this earnest desire for peace, rash and intemperate language used on both sides led to a temporary rupture between the two great leaders. In 1741 Wesley records: "Whitefield told me he and I preached two different Gospels, and therefore he not only would not join with or give me the right hand of fellowship but was resolved to preach publicly against me and my brother wheresoever he preached at all."[1] Fortunately, through the true spirit of charity and forbearance displayed by both, the quarrel was of short duration, as Whitefield writes in the following year, "Let us bear and forbear one another in love. God be praised for giving you such a mind"; and in 1748, "I rejoice to hear that you and your brother are more moderate with respect to *sinless perfection* . . . as for *universal redemption*, if we omit on each side the talking for or against reprobation . . . and agree, as we already do, in giving an universal offer to all poor sinners that will come and taste of the waters of life, I think we may manage very well. . . . I cannot agree with you in some principles, but that need not hinder love, since I trust we hold the foundation, even 'Jesus, the same yesterday, to-day, and for ever.'"[2]

This friendly attitude was always after maintained. On one occasion Whitefield was asked "whether he thought they would see John Wesley in heaven?" "No, sir," he replied, "I fear not. He will be so near the throne, and we at such a distance, that we shall hardly get a sight of him;"[3] and in his will he left a mourning ring to John and Charles Wesley, "in token of my indissoluble union with them in heart and Christian affection, notwithstanding our difference in Judgement about some particular points of doctrine."[4]

Unfortunately the controversy was renewed with far greater bitterness in 1771 with the publication of the *Minutes of the Methodist Conference of 1770*. The doctrines propounded by these were pronounced "a dreadful heresy" by Lady Huntingdon and her Calvinistic adherents, and certainly were somewhat inconsistent with Wesley's previous views on Justification. In 1739 he had declared: "I believe neither our own holiness nor good works are any part of the cause of our justification. . . . I believe no good work can be previous to justification, nor consequently a condition of it, but that we are justified by faith alone, faith without works, faith (though producing all, yet) including no good

[1] *Journal*, March 28.
[2] Andrews, pp. 168 and 210.
[3] Ryle, *Christian Leaders*, p. 60.
[4] Gillies (*ante*), p. 355.

work."[1] Yet one of the Minutes of 1770 stated: "In fact, every believer, till he comes to glory, works for as well as *from* life."[2]

The Calvinists insisted on a formal recantation of the obnoxious Minutes, and Wesley wrote to Lady Huntingdon requesting that the Minutes might be referred to his *Sermons on Salvation by Faith*, published in 1738, and at the next Conference he and his preachers generously signed a declaration stating that "as the Minutes have been understood to favour justification by works, we declare we had no such meaning, and that we abhor the doctrine of justification by works as a most perilous and abominable doctrine . . . we declare we have no trust but in the merits of Christ for justification or salvation. And though no one is a real Christian believer who doth not good works when there is time or opportunity, yet our works have no part in meriting or purchasing our justification from first to last, in whole or in part."[3]

The storm, however, had not yet blown over, although the Calvinists professed themselves satisfied with the declaration. Fletcher of Madeley felt it necessary to write his *Checks to Antinomianism* in vindication of the Minutes. This led to violent and abusive replies from the Calvinistic protagonists—in fact, the excited zeal and intensity of conviction of the combatants on both sides showed a sad lack of Christian charity and self-control. They were both contending with great vehemence for opposite sides of truth. The Arminians were insistent on the universality of God's grace and the necessity of Christian morality, while the Calvinists were equally tenacious for the doctrines of Divine sovereignty and the unmerited forgiveness of God, and thus they each failed to see the question from their opponents' point of view.

The most able but, it must be confessed, the most acrimonious disputant on the Calvinistic side was Augustus Toplady (1740–78). In 1774 he published *The Historic Proof of the Doctrinal Calvinism of the Church of England*, a book which displayed his undoubted ability and scholarship, and which a modern bishop asserted "was never answered because it was unanswerable."[4] It is, however, almost unaccountable that the author of "Rock of Ages," who in his private and pastoral life as Vicar of Broad Hembury was most diligent and exemplary and universally beloved, should, in his controversial writings, have used most

[1] *Journal*, Sept. 13. [2] *Wesley's Designated Successor*, p. 170.
[3] *Life and Times of Countess of Huntingdon*, ii. 170.
[4] Ryle (*ante*), p. 380.

unpardonably bitter and uncharitable language towards his opponents.

Fortunately the heat of the controversy did not last long, and many of the participants in it lived to lament their intemperate language, and although for a while it divided friends and seriously hindered the cause of the Revival, yet as time went on it was more and more discountenanced, and the later Evangelicals, whether of Calvinistic or Arminian opinions, worked harmoniously side by side. Thus Henry Venn replied once to an inquiry if a certain young minister was a Calvinist or Arminian: "I really do not know. He is a sincere disciple of the Lord Jesus Christ, and that is of infinitely more importance than his being a disciple of Calvin or Arminius."[1] The celebrated Charles Simeon also tritely remarked: "Both of them (Calvinists and Arminians) are right in all they affirm and wrong in all they deny. The Calvinist wishes for some texts to be expunged from Scripture, the Arminian wishes the same as to others. . . . I wish for all the Bible to remain as it is." And he adds: "In Scripture there are Calvinistic principles to act on man's hopes, and Arminian principles to act on his fears; both are needful and combine to produce the right effect."[2]

CHAPTER IX

THE RISE OF THE EVANGELICALS

It has been well remarked that "the failure of a prudential system of ethics as a restraining force upon society was perceived or felt, in the way of reaction, by the Evangelical and Methodist generation of teachers who succeeded the Hanoverian divines."[3] We have already traced the course of this reaction in the distinctly Methodist phase of the Revival movement; it is therefore time now to consider the rise and influence of an increasing number of parochial clergy, in full sympathy with this great religious awakening, who soon acquired the sobriquet of "Evan-

[1] Venn's *Complete Duty of Man*, Preface, p. xv. (1841).

[2] Brown, *Recollections of Simeon's Conversation Parties*, pp. 267–74 (1863).

[3] *Essays and Reviews*, p. 326.

gelicals." It was the revival of an old name which had at first been used to describe the early adherents of the Reformed opinions in England, and now began to be applied as a term of contempt to those clergy who taught the doctrines of the Revival, but does not appear to have been claimed by them until towards the close of the century, when its use became general. In the early stages of the Revival the title "Methodist" was indiscriminately applied in derision to all who were tainted with "enthusiasm," even if they were in no way associated with the work of Wesley or Whitefield; but, although too often confounded, there was a distinct difference between the "Evangelical" clergy and the Wesleyan Methodists. It is therefore necessary, in order to prevent a misapprehension of terms, to consider the precise connotation of the title "Evangelical," and it is well here to correct a very popular misconception in the present day which has led to a confusion of Evangelicals with Low Churchmen. However similar the two parties may have become to-day, originally the Low Churchmen were the strongest opponents of the teachings of the revivalists, whether Evangelicals or Methodists. In the eighteenth century Low Churchmanship was practically synonymous with the Latitudinarian theology so specially obnoxious to the Evangelicals. Thus there must have been a certain foundation of truth in the satirical description given by Sacheverell, the famous Tory High Churchman, in 1702. "We will sum up," he says, "the articles of a Low Churchman's creed. . . . He believes very little or no Revelation, and had rather lay his faith upon the substantial Evidence of his own Reason than the precarious Authority of Divine Testimony. . . . He had rather be a Deist, Socinian, or Nestorian than affront his own Understanding with believing what is incomprehensible, or be so rude as to obtrude on others what he himself cannot explain. He thinks the Articles of the Church too stiff, formal, and strait-laced a Rule to confine his Faith in. . . . He looks upon the censuring of False Doctrine as a Dogmatical Usurpation, an intrusion upon that human liberty which he sets up as the measure and extent of his belief. He makes the most of this World, being not over confident of any Other." [1]

Although the Evangelicals were not diametrically opposed to the Methodists, as they were to the Low Churchmen, yet they usually repudiated the term as applied to themselves, because it too often conveyed a false impression of their principles or

[1] Sacheverell's *Character of a Low Churchman*, p. 5 (1706).

teaching. It is true that they were often indebted to Methodist influence, if not for their actual conversion, at least for greater spiritual zeal or inspiration, and although several of the early Evangelical clergy actively associated themselves with the evangelistic labours of Wesley or Whitefield, yet as a body they differed materially from the doctrines or methods of both these great leaders. As the great majority of the Evangelicals held the moderate Calvinistic opinions so dear to Whitefield, they were opposed to the Arminian teaching of Wesley and his followers, and they still more objected to the flagrant disregard of the parochial system which was so conspicuous a feature of Wesley and the Methodists generally.

It was, in fact, this latter practice which soon became the virtual dividing line between Methodists and Evangelicals. The contempt for Church orders and discipline and the irregular conduct of the Methodist preachers soon convinced the parochial clergy in sympathy with them of the inevitable tendency of the movement, once the restraining hand of its great leader was removed. Even Berridge, the original and erratic vicar of Everton, and one of Lady Huntingdon's chaplains, had forewarned her of the dangers of schism. "What will become," he writes in 1777, "of your students at your decease? They are virtual Dissenters, and will be settled Dissenters then. And the same will happen to many, perhaps most, of Mr. Wesley's preachers at his death. He rules like a real Alexander and is now stepping forth like a flaming torch, but we do not read in history of two Alexanders succeeding each other." [1] The Evangelical also formed a striking contrast to the Wesleyan Methodist movement in its want of any definite organisation. It was not kept together by devoted allegiance to any one supreme leader; in fact, it exerted no united action beyond that of friends and fellow clergy who preached the same doctrines; and thus the progress of the movement, if such it can be termed, has to be sought rather in its effect and outcome from the lives and work of its individual leaders than in the growth of any special system or society.

Although the theological views of the Evangelicals were largely in accord with the works of the Reformers of the sixteenth and the Puritan theology of the seventeenth century, yet Evangelicalism was not merely a revival of Puritanism. Much of their inspiration and fervent zeal for the salvation of souls may have

[1] *Life and Times of Lady Huntingdon*, ii. 423.

been derived from Puritan teaching, and they certainly resembled the Puritans in their supreme veneration for Holy Scripture and in their love for Bible phraseology, but here the similarity ceased. "The typical Puritan," it has been well stated, "was gloomy and austere; the typical Evangelical was bright and genial. The Puritan would not be kept *within* the pale of the National Church; the Evangelical would not be kept *out* of it. The Puritan was dissatisfied with our liturgy, our ceremonies, our vestments, and our hierarchy; the Evangelical was not only perfectly contented with every one of these things, but was ready to contend for them all as heartily as the highest of High Churchmen. . . . The Puritans were frequently in antagonism with 'the powers that be,' the Evangelicals never; no amount of ill-treatment could put them out of love with our constitution both in Church and State."[1] It was this firm attachment to the Church and to definite Church principles which soon so conspicuously separated them from the followers of Wesley or the adherents of the Countess of Huntingdon's "Connexion," whose methods were rapidly carrying them into the ranks of the Dissenters. Although the deplorable ignorance and godlessness of the people, especially in the numerous districts where the clergy were either non-resident or scandalously incapable through drunkenness or worldliness, impelled several of the earlier Evangelicals to carry the Gospel message to those outside the boundaries of their own parishes, yet this practice in no way affected their love for Church order and discipline, and many of them in their later years regretted even this pardonable irregularity.

Thus Grimshaw of Haworth, a conspicuous offender in this direction, encouraged his own flock to gather together for a daily early morning service at 5 a.m., and wrote to Charles Wesley that "he believed the Church of England to be the soundest, purest, and most apostolical, well-constituted national Christian church in the world."[2] The communicants in his church were so numerous that Wesley, who preached there in 1757, records that "I suppose we had near a thousand communicants, and scarce a trifler among them,"[3] and on a subsequent occasion he declared that "the communicants alone filled the church."

The Evangelicals had an intense affection for the Homilies and Articles, and above all for the Liturgy of the Church, which they strove to have performed in a devout and orderly manner.

[1] Overton, *Eng. Ch. in 18th Cent.*, p. 315.
[2] Hardy's *Life of Grimshaw*, p. 174 (1860). [3] *Journal*, May 22.

We are told that Romaine "took great pains to have th services of his church conducted with strict reverence and goo order," [1] while Charles Simeon was convinced "that the deadnes and formality experienced in the worship of the Church arise far more from the low state of our graces than from any defect i our Liturgy. If only we had our hearts deeply penitent an contrite, I know from my experience at this hour that no prayer in the world could be better suited to our wants or more delightfu to our souls." [2] "Never do I find myself nearer to God," h declared on another occasion, "than I often am in the readin desk." "The purest sight short of heaven would be a whol congregation using the prayers of the Liturgy in the true spirit o them." [3]

It was not altogether unnatural that, at a time when almost al the popular amusements were associated with some form of si or immorality, and mainly patronised by people conspicuous fo the looseness and impiety of their lives, the Evangelicals shoul encourage a rigid and somewhat ascetic life, and vigorously ba the theatre, the dance, and the card table ; yet there is somethin beautifully fascinating in the regularity and simplicity of thei everyday conduct. Possibly no better description of this can b found than that given by the celebrated Evangelical poet, Willian Cowper. "As to amusements," he writes, "we have none. Th place indeed swarms with them, and cards and dancing are th professed business of almost all the gentle inhabitants of Hunt ingdon. We refuse to take part in them, or to be accessories t this way of murdering our time, and by so doing have acquire the name of Methodists. . . . We breakfast commonly betwee eight and nine ; till eleven we read either the Scriptures, or th sermons of some faithful preacher of those holy mysteries at eleven we attend divine service, which is performed her twice daily ; and from twelve to three we separate and amus ourselves as we please. During that interval I either read i my own apartment, or walk, or ride, or work in the garden we seldom sit an hour after dinner, but if the weather permits adjourn to the garden, where, with Mrs. Unwin and her son, have generally the pleasure of religious conversation till tea-time If it rains or is too windy for walking, we either converse withi doors or sing some hymns of Martin's collection. . . . After te we sally forth to walk in good earnest. . . . At night we read o

[1] Ryle (*ante*), p. 169. [2] Carus, *Life of Simeon*, p. 17 (1848).
[3] Moule's *Life of Simeon*, p. 108.

converse as before till supper, and commonly finish the evening either with hymns or a sermon, and last of all the family are called to prayers. I need not tell *you* that such a life as this is consistent with the utmost cheerfulness; accordingly we are all happy, and dwell together in unity as brethren." [1]

The truths taught by the Evangelical clergy were no new doctrines, but simply those which, owing to the Latitudinarian and philosophical spirit of the age, had been largely neglected and which were now revived with all the vigour and freshness of fervent evangelistic preaching. They strongly insisted on the distinctive foundation truths of Christianity—the guilt and depravity of human nature owing to the fall of man, his utter inability to turn to God by his own efforts, the full and complete redemption wrought for mankind by Christ's death on the Cross, the benefit of which is appropriated by faith alone; the renewing and sanctifying work of the Holy Spirit, displayed in personal holiness of life, the only true evidence of a real change of heart. In order to maintain their influence over their converts, they generally adopted the Methodist plan of forming them into Societies, meeting at regular intervals, for mutual instruction and edification. They also followed the example of the Methodists in substituting congregational hymn-singing for the old metrical versions of the psalms, which were at this time generally sung by the choir alone in a slovenly, irreverent manner, while the rest of the congregation remained seated.

It must be admitted that the Evangelicals were often too censorious in their dealings with those differing from their own special theological views, and, it may be, too little appreciative of work not undertaken exactly on their own lines. They were also inclined to adopt a set phraseology which was often unintelligible to those out of sympathy with their religious ideals and opinions, but the reality of their own spiritual experience and the intensity of their convictions largely accounted for their narrow outlook or lack of charity. Their religion was everything to them, and the disinterested zeal, the intense earnestness, and the conspicuous clearness with which they presented the truths of the Gospel won the admiration, and often overcame the prejudices, of those opposed to their theology; and certainly formed a striking contrast to the worldly, self-seeking aims of the majority of the so-called "orthodox" divines of the period, who possessed a supreme contempt for anything akin to "enthusiasm." A

[1] *Cowper's Letters*, p. 12 (World's Classics).

weighty authority has declared that "they were the salt of the earth in their day; that their disinterestedness, their moral courage in braving obloquy and unpopularity, their purity of life, the spirituality of their teaching, and the world of practical good they did among a neglected people, rendered them worthy of the deepest respect." [1]

CHAPTER X

PROMINENT EVANGELICAL CLERGY

(*a*) *The Pioneers*

Of the parochial clergy who from the first actively furthered the cause of the Evangelical revival, none is more worthy to be remembered than John William Fletcher (1729–85), who was for twenty-five years vicar of the large village of Madeley in Shropshire. "Never perhaps since the rise of Christianity has 'the mind which was in Christ Jesus' been more faithfully copied than it was in the vicar of Madeley." [2] "No age or country," says Southey, "has produced a man of more fervent piety, or more perfect charity; no Church has ever possessed a more apostolic minister." [3]

A native of Switzerland, and originally intended for the ministry of the Swiss Reformed Church, as a young man Fletcher visited England for the purpose of acquiring the language, and soon after obtained the post of private tutor to a Mr. Hill, a Shropshire gentleman. It was while here that his serious demeanour attracted the attention of Mrs. Hill, who observed, "I shall wonder if our tutor does not turn Methodist by-and-by." "Methodist, madam," said he, "pray, what is that?" "Why, the Methodists are a people that do nothing but pray." "Are they?" said he. "Then, by the help of God, I will find them out, if they be above ground." [4]

After passing through a long period of great mental and

[1] Overton, *Eng. Ch. in 18th Cent.*, p. 402.
[2] Overton, *Eng. Ch.* &c., p. 343. [3] *Life of Wesley*, p. 282.
[4] *Wesley's Designated Successor*, pp. 14–16.

spiritual struggle, he confesses to finding relief by reading Wesley's *Journal,* "when I heard that we should not build on what we feel, but go to Christ with all our sins and all our hardness of heart."[1]

In spite of the fact that he was not a British subject, and apparently had no prospect of any definite parochial work, he was ordained in 1757, and frequently preached for John Wesley and also in several of Lady Huntingdon's chapels. In 1760 his patron Mr. Hill offered him the living of Dunham, which he refused because the population was too small and the income too large! He was willing, however, to accept that of Madeley, where the conditions were exactly reversed, and his patron found no difficulty in persuading the vicar to exchange that living for Dunham, which was worth twice as much. Thus he found himself in charge of a large parish consisting mainly of colliers and forgemen. He described the bulk of the inhabitants as "stupid heathens, who seemed past all curiosity, as well as all sense of godliness." Wesley sought to persuade him that his calling was that of an itinerating evangelist and that this living was merely "the snare of the devil to him,"[2] but his future work at Madeley proved the wisdom of his choice. Although he met with very great difficulties, and was much discouraged at first by his small congregations and the apparent fruitlessness of his labours, his transparent zeal and consistent witness before long began to make an impression on his godless parishioners. One manifest sign of this was the persecution which he soon had to endure from those whose shameless lives were exposed and reproved by his faithful ministry. Many refused to admit him to their houses and even to pay the tithes owing to him, while they used every effort to turn him out of his cure. But Fletcher was not the man to be daunted by opposition, and he continued to rebuke all kinds of vice and sin. He would frequently burst in upon midnight gatherings of drunken revellers, and disperse them with stern words of warning, so that he soon became the terror of all the evil-doers in the neighbourhood.

In 1768, in addition to his arduous parochial labours, he undertook the post of visitor to Lady Huntingdon's college at Trevecca, which he held till the unfortunate Calvinistic dispute led to his resignation. "It is impossible," wrote Dr. Benson, the head-master, "for me to describe the veneration in which we all held him. Like Elijah in the schools of the Prophets, he was

[1] Ibid. [2] Ibid., pp. 58–9.

revered, loved, and almost adored. . . . His life from day to day *was hid with Christ in God.*" [1]

In 1776 his unceasing energies led to a complete breakdown of his weak constitution, and one who visited him during his long illness of five years records: "I went to see a man who had one foot in the grave, but I found a man who had one foot in heaven."

After his death, John Wesley, who had known him intimately for thirty years, declared "that he did not expect to find another so unblamable a character—one so inwardly and outwardly devoted to God—on this side eternity." On one occasion, when solicited whether any preferment would be acceptable to him in return for the important services he had rendered the Government by his writings on the American Rebellion, this humble-minded saint answered, "I want nothing but more grace," [2]

James Hervey (1714–58) had been one of the original members of the little band of Oxford Methodists, but even if his very delicate health had not made it impossible, his strict views of Church order would have prevented his adopting the irregular itinerating methods of his early teacher. He spent his short, blameless life almost entirely at Weston Favell, near Northampton first as curate for his father and then as rector. He lived a quiet, earnest, useful life as a faithful country parson. He was the author of *Meditations among the Tombs* and *Theron and Aspasio*, two books which were for many years exceedingly popular, although written in a peculiar bombastic style which would be anything but acceptable to-day.[3] But the entire proceeds of his literary labours, besides a great part of his small income, was regularly devoted to charitable purposes, and his sole aim both in his preaching and writing was to "recommend his dear Redeemer." Even on the day of his death, although in great pain, he persisted in exhorting his doctor to attend to his eternal welfare. "No," said he, "Doctor, no; you tell me I have but a few moments to live. O! let me spend them in adoring our great Redeemer." [4]

The career of William Grimshaw (1708–63) forms a striking

[1] *Life and Times of Countess of Huntingdon*, ii. 102.

[2] *Wesley's Designated Successor*, p. 353.

[3] *Theron and Aspasio*, his famous dialogue vindicating the doctrine of justification by faith in the imputed righteousness of Christ, passed through three editions in one year.

[4] Hervey's Works, vol. i. p. xiii. (1789).

contrast to that of Hervey. If Hervey's life speaks to us of the sweet soft music which charms and soothes, Grimshaw's resembles rather the rough hammer that breaks and bruises; but his was just the character suited to deal with the rough and almost heathenish inhabitants of the wild and desolate village of Haworth in Yorkshire, of which he was perpetual curate 1742–63. In his early ministerial career he had been careless and indifferent. "He refrained as much as possible from gross swearing unless in suitable company, and, when he got drunk, would take care to sleep it out before he came home."[1] But the effect of his mother's death brought about an entire change, and his robust piety soon began to transform Haworth and the surrounding neighbourhood. The Sunday football matches were stopped and the church became crowded with devout and earnest worshippers. Grimshaw is even credited with leaving just before the sermon, riding-whip in hand, in order to drive into the church the Sunday morning loafers from the public-house. Services were held in outlying barns for those who complained that they could not get to church, and he divided his large parish into twelve districts, in which he held monthly visitations to inquire into the spiritual state of those who gathered to meet him. His unconventional methods were well suited to the character of his flock; yet "in the performance of divine service, and especially in the Communion," we are told, "he was at times like a man with his feet on earth and his soul in heaven."[2]

His influence and energy were so great that he found it impossible to confine himself to the limits of his own parish, and extended his evangelistic labours into the neighbouring counties, where he formed his converts into societies under local leaders. These irregular methods caused him to be greatly disliked by many of the neighbouring clergy, and complaints were often made to the Archbishop of his extra-parochial labours. "How many communicants had you when you came to Haworth?" asked the Archbishop. "Twelve, my lord," replied Grimshaw. "How many have you now?" "In the winter from three to four hundred, in the summer near twelve hundred." "We cannot find fault with Mr. Grimshaw," said the Archbishop, "when he is instrumental in bringing so many persons to the Lord's Table."[3]

One of the best known and certainly the most eccentric of the

[1] Middleton, *Biographia Evangelica*, iv. 398 (1786). [2] Ibid., iv. 403.
[3] Hardy's *Life of Grimshaw*, p. 232.

earlier Evangelicals was the clever and humorous John Berridge (1716–93), who sacrificed an easy and comfortable position as senior Fellow of Clare Hall, Cambridge, for a strenuous life as vicar of Everton in Bedfordshire. Although a ripe scholar, his preaching seemed specially suited to the ignorant rustics in the agricultural districts where he laboured, and was at first accompanied (like that of Wesley's) by mysterious physical or hysterical symptoms of religious frenzy. Berridge, however, in no way encouraged these unaccountable outbreaks, and in time they entirely disappeared. His success and popularity as an evangelist in the surrounding districts was even greater than that of Grimshaw, and thousands flocked to hear him wherever he preached. The Bishop urged him to desist from this irregular practice, but he refused to promise not to enter other men's parishes, saying that "if they would preach the Gospel themselves, there would be no need for my preaching it to their people, but as they do not, I cannot desist."[1] It was only the intervention of his old college friend, the Earl of Chatham, that prevented the Bishop proceeding against him for his disobedience. The quaint epitaph which he composed for his own tombstone was thoroughly typical of this pious but eccentric servant of God:—

> Reader, art thou born again?
> No salvation without a new birth!
> I was born in sin February 1716.
> Remained ignorant of my fallen state till 1730.
> Lived proudly on faith and works for salvation till 1754.
> Was admitted to Everton vicarage 1751.
> Fled to Jesus alone for refuge 1756.
> Fell asleep in Christ, January 22, 1793.

One of the foremost of the Evangelical clergy was Henry Venn (1724–97), an illustrious representative of a deeply interesting family which, in every generation since the Reformation, has given a son to the ministry of the Church. His real life-work was done as vicar of the important living of Huddersfield, 1759–71. His evangelistic labours, both in his own large parish and in the neighbourhood, were incessant, and his influence and power as a preacher truly remarkable. "As soon as he began to preach," his son, John Venn, records, "the church became crowded to such an extent that many were not able to procure admission. Numbers became deeply impressed with concern

[1] Ryle (*ante*), pp. 232–5.

about their immortal souls ; persons flocked from distant hamlets, inquiring what they must do to be saved." [1] Simeon wrote to his grandson in 1833 : " I wish you had known your grandfather. The only end for which he lived was to make all men see the glory of God in the face of Jesus Christ." [2] He was intimately connected with the great evangelists Wesley and Whitefield, and frequently preached for Lady Huntingdon. In 1771 overwork compelled him to seek the quiet retirement of the country living of Yelling, near Cambridge, where for many years the old soldier of the Cross, who had almost finished his course, influenced by his correspondence, his spiritual counsel and inspiration, the younger men who were just entering the battle. Amongst these was Charles Simeon, who records that " in this aged minister I found a father, an instructor, and a most bright example, and I shall have reason to adore my God to all eternity for the benefit of his acquaintance." [3] He was the author of *The Complete Duty of Man*, an able doctrinal treatise, dealing with practical Christian duties, the fruit of his own ministerial experience, which was widely popular for many years. It was chiefly intended to correct the defective theological teaching of the famous seventeenth century production *The Whole Duty of Man*, which Cowper described as " that repository of self-righteousness and pharisaical lumber." [4]

Probably the most attractive, and certainly the most romantic, character connected with the Evangelical revival is that of John Newton (1725–1807), who in his early years had become an infidel through reading the writings of Shaftesbury, and in his wild roving life as sailor and slave-dealer had, on his own confession, fallen into the lowest depths of sin and degradation. " Perhaps the history of the whole Church," he wrote, " does not afford an instance of one so totally abandoned, being called to preach the gospel." [5] " I not only sinned with a high hand myself, but made it my study to tempt and seduce others upon every occasion." In the midst of his profligate career, however, his early religious impressions and his fidelity to a youthful love always acted as a restraining influence, and the experience of a dangerous storm at sea eventually led to a thorough change of life. He had always possessed a singular thirst for knowledge,

[1] *Venn Family Annals*, p. 80 (1904).
[2] Carus, *Life of Simeon*, p. 502. [3] Ibid., p. 26.
[4] Southey's *Life of Cowper*, i. 81 (1854).
[5] J. Bull, *Life of Newton*, p. 195.

and he now rapidly educated himself till he became more than an average scholar, and in 1764 succeeded in getting ordained as curate of the little town of Olney in Buckinghamshire, where he used every effort, by numerous Sunday and weekday services, to influence his poor, starving parishioners. He was most effective, however, in dealing with individual souls, whether by correspondence or personal intercourse. His affectionate nature and his personal experience of the sins and temptations of life, combined with his own marvellous conversion, gave hope to the most abandoned sinner. In 1780 he accepted the living of St. Mary Woolnoth, London, but it was at Olney that, in conjunction with Cowper, he composed a set of hymns, many of which, like " How sweet the name of Jesus sounds," " Come, my soul, thy suit prepare," " Hark, my soul, it is the Lord," " God moves in a mysterious way." " There is a fountain filled with Blood," are still justly esteemed and very generally used.

In writing of Newton we are led by a natural sequence to the pathetic but fascinating character of his great friend William Cowper, the Olney poet, who, a well-informed writer has asserted, " contributed more in his way towards the spread of the Evangelical revival than even Whitefield or Wesley." [1] Certainly the recognised wit and genius of the lyrics of this cultured and retiring poet must have removed the prejudices of many against the Evangelical doctrines which were so dear to him. There is a peculiar attractiveness in his unobtrusive and poetic presentation of evangelical truth :—

" I was a stricken deer that left the herd
Long since ; with many an arrow deep infix'd
My panting side was charged, when I withdrew
To seek a tranquil death in distant shades.
There was I found by One who had Himself
Been hurt by the archers. In His side He bore,
And in His hands and feet, the cruel scars.
With gentle force soliciting the darts,
He drew them forth and heal'd and bade me live." [2]

Cowper's poetry, with its fervent yet practical piety, its thorough knowledge of human nature, and its clever and fearless exposure of the vices and corruptions of society and the terrible decay of national virtue, did untold good to the cause of real spiritual

[1] Overton, *Eng. Ch.*, &c., p. 381.
[2] *The Task* (Poetical Works, p. 257).

religion, and gained an entrance into circles where the influence or eloquence of the Evangelists could never have penetrated.

The only Evangelical clergyman working in London till nearly the close of the century was the celebrated William Romaine (1714–95), the author of *The Life, Walk, and Triumph of Faith,* who had gained while at Oxford a very considerable reputation for his great learning. His ministerial career in the metropolis is a conspicuous example of the persistent and scandalous persecution which the earlier Evangelicals often encountered. Appointed afternoon lecturer at St. Dunstan's in 1749, not only his doctrines, but the large congregations he attracted, soon excited the opposition of the vicar and churchwardens, who endeavoured to deprive him of his position. Failing in this, they altered the hour of his lecture, and refused to open the doors a minute before the time, or even to light and warm the church, so that Romaine was frequently compelled to preach by the aid of a single lighted taper. At length the Bishop interfered to prevent this outrageous treatment, but Romaine met with similar experiences in several other lectureships he held at different times, nearly all of which he was soon forced to resign. At St. George's, Hanover Square, the parishioners complained because the numbers of the poorer classes attracted by his preaching caused them inconvenience; although the Earl of Northampton well remarked: "If the power to attract be imputed as matter of admiration to Garrick, why should it be urged as a crime against Romaine? Shall excellence be considered exceptional only in Divine things?"[1] At length in 1764 this opposition ceased, when he gained the independent position of Rector of St. Andrew's, Blackfriars, where he worked with conspicuous success for thirty years. On his first Good Friday the communicants numbered five hundred, and at his death the esteem in which he was generally held was evidenced by the immense crowd of all classes which attended his funeral, headed by the City Marshals. "He lived," says his biographer, "more with God than with men, and to know his real history, or the best part of it, it would be requisite to know what passed between God and his soul."[2]

By far the most famous advocate of Evangelical doctrines in Wales was Daniel Rowlands (1713–90), who for thirty years was curate of Llangeitho, first to his brother and then to his son. His extraordinary power as a preacher almost rivalled that of

[1] Ryle (*ante*), p. 160. [2] Cadogan's *Life of Romaine*, p. 73 (1796).

Whitefield; people flocked from all parts of the Principality to hear him, and he often had as many as two thousand communicants on Sundays. His popularity was immense, and he evangelised in almost every part of Wales, and established a regular system of societies connected with one central association. This itinerant preaching was strongly resented by the worldly and indolent clergy by whom he was surrounded. Consequently, in 1763, the Bishop most unwisely withdrew his licence; an action which he afterwards bitterly regretted, as, in spite of Rowlands' dying advice "to stand by the Church by all means," [1] the majority of his large following seceded from it and laid the foundation of the Welsh Calvinistic Methodist body.

If space permitted, the labours of other prominent Evangelicals might be recorded, such as Walker of Truro (1714–61), whose wonderful life and personality entirely changed the character of his parish, or Thomas Adam of Winteringham (1701–84), who was regarded as a sort of oracle by his fellow Evangelicals; but the remarkable feature to be borne in mind in regard to these early pioneers is the wonderful extent of their influence in proportion to their numbers and the positions they occupied. Although quite an insignificant portion of clergy and scarcely possessing one really important town living, scattered as they were throughout the country, the wonderful effect of their lives and work radiated from their village rectories to almost every part of England and Wales.

The opposition and strong prejudice entertained against Evangelical teaching was persistent and widespread during the earlier years of the Revival, and most of the early leaders of the movement encountered their share of persecution, but it was at the Universities where this antagonistic spirit was carried to the greatest lengths. The Evangelicals fared specially badly at Oxford, and a most disgraceful case of intolerant persecution occurred in connection with seven "Methodist" students of St. Edmund Hall, in 1768, who were accused of "talking of regeneration, inspiration, and drawing nigh to God." The Vice-Chancellor actually consented to hold a Court of Inquiry into the case, and in spite of the strong protest of Dr. Dixon, the Principal of the Hall, who declared that their opinions were orthodox and their lives most exemplary, six of the "Methodist" undergraduates were expelled from the University as "enemies of the Church and frequenters of an illegal conventicle," because

[1] Owen's *Memoir of Rowlands*, p. 236 (1840).

hey had presumed to attend drawing-room meetings for extem-orary prayer and the study of the Scriptures." [1]

(*b*) *The Second Generation*

As the century drew to a close there was a distinct change in the ethods and attitude of the Evangelical clergy. Nearly all he early pioneers had been intimately associated with the ork of Wesley and Whitefield or had acted as chaplains for he Countess of Huntingdon, while several of them had adopted he distinctively Methodist practice of itinerant evangelisation. he later Evangelicals, on the other hand, entirely separated hemselves from the Methodist organisation, and distinctly dis-pproved of irregular extra-parochial labours or similar breaches f Church order and discipline. Thus Hannah More recorded ith satisfaction "that she had never been present at a con-enticle or entered one of the 'Tabernacles' like Moorfields, here the Methodists conducted their services." [2] Even Henry enn in his old age lamented the irregular practices he had ndulged in while at Huddersfield, and did his best to restrain thers from following his example; [3] while Simeon declared that he was hardly satisfied that Berridge was doing right in preach-ng from place to place." He admitted that "he lived when isorder was needful," but added, "To do *now* as he did *then* ould do much harm." [4]

The latter end of the century witnessed a large increase in he number of the Evangelical clergy, and also the removal, o a certain extent, of the general antipathy in which they had een previously held. One of the clearest evidences of this hange was seen in the secure footing which they at length btained in the Universities, and more especially at Cambridge. s late as 1779 the prejudice against Evangelicals had been o strong that Henry Venn found some difficulty in getting his on admitted to a Cambridge college, but about ten years later here was quite a celebrated knot of men, connected with the overning bodies of the various colleges, who were in sympathy ith Evangelical teaching. One of the most prominent of these as Isaac Milner (1750–1820), President of Queen's College,

[1] *Cf.* Balleine, *Hist. of Evang. Party*, p. 124.
[2] Tytler, *Countess of Huntingdon and her Circle*, p. 29.
[3] *Cf.* Venn's *Complete Duty of Man*, p. xiii., preface 3.
[4] *Recollections of Simeon's Conversation Parties*, p. 200.

and also, after 1791, Dean of Carlisle. His great reputatio as a scholar—for he had been Senior Wrangler and First Smith Prizeman—gained him general respect; while his influenti position and his determined yet genial spirit soon overcam the aversion entertained for his theological views, and befor long he made Queen's College the recognised stronghold fc men of Evangelical opinions.

Two other zealous supporters of the Evangelical cause, almos equally as brilliant in intellectual attainments as Milner, wer William Farish, Fellow of Magdalene and Professor of Chemistry and Joseph Jowett, Fellow of Trinity Hall and Regius Professo of Civil Law; but the man who exercised the widest and mos permanent influence on University life was Charles Simeo (1759–1836), Fellow of King's College. Commencing his Uni versity career as a vain and thoughtless undergraduate, his min had been turned in a serious direction through the obligatio of attending the Communion Service in his College Chapel Realising his unpreparedness, he sought help from religiou books, and at length, while reading Bishop Wilson's book o the Lord's Supper, he realised the full purpose of the Atone ment. "The thought rushed into my mind," he says, "What may I transfer all my guilt to another? Has God provided a Offering for me, that I may lay my sins on His head? Then God willing, I will not bear them on my own soul one momen longer."[1]

In 1783 Simeon was appointed incumbent of Trinity Church but his decided Evangelical preaching soon brought him int conflict with his congregation, and for many years he had t endure petty acts of persecution of the most unwarrantable an distressing character. His services were interrupted by rowdy bands of undergraduates, and the seat-holders locked up thei pews, and the forms, provided in the aisles for the accommoda tion of the congregation, were thrown into the churchyard Simeon had also started the unprecedented "innovation" o an evening service, which was largely attended; but the church wardens soon stopped this by locking the church doors. Gradu ally, however, his quiet, firm, and patient persistence overcame all opposition, and at length he became universally respected as one of the greatest spiritual forces in the University. His conversational Bible classes were especially popular amongst undergraduates, and his sermon classes greatly valued by

[1] Carus (*ante*), p. 16.

rdination candidates. An intimate friend and contemporary, peaking of his wonderful life and influence, says, "Never did see such consistency and reality of devotion, such warmth of iety, such zeal and love"; [1] while Macaulay wrote in 1844, 'As to Simeon, if you knew what his authority and influence vere, and how they extended from Cambridge to the most remote orners of England, you would allow that his real sway over the hurch was far greater than that of any Primate." [2]

Another sign of the increasing strength of the Evangelicals was the number of influential positions they held in London towards the close of the century. Romaine in his latter years was surrounded by quite a small circle of sympathetic lecturers, or incumbents of the proprietary chapels, which at first furnished more accessible spheres of influence for the Evangelical clergy than the regular parishes. In 1779 John Newton had come to St. Mary Woolnoth. Dr. Haweis was at the Lock Chapel and Basil Woodd at Bentinck Chapel, but probably the two most noted representatives of Evangelicalism in London were Thomas Scott, who came as morning preacher at the Lock Chapel in 1785, and the cultured Richard Cecil, who was incumbent of St. John's, Bedford Row, proprietary chapel, 1780–1808. Scott had in many ways a remarkable career. He entered the ministry, he admits in his striking little autobiography *The Force of Truth*, entirely from worldly motives of self-advantage, as he declared that "I was nearly a Socinian and Pelagian and wholly an Arminian, yet I sought to obtain admission into the ministry in a church whose doctrines are diametrically opposed to all three." "With a heart full of pride and wickedness . . . after having subscribed articles directly contrary to what I believed, and after having blasphemously declared . . . that I judged myself to be inwardly moved by the Holy Ghost to take that office upon me (not knowing or believing that there was a Holy Ghost) on Sept. 20, 1772, I was ordained a deacon." [3]

A few years later he was brought into contact with Newton at Olney, and endeavoured to turn him from his "Methodistical" opinions. A long correspondence was commenced between them, and Scott had "no inconsiderable expectations that his arguments would prove irresistibly convincing and he would have the honour of rescuing a well-meaning person from his enthusiastical

[1] Moule's *Life of Simeon*, p. 82.
[2] Trevelyan, *Life of Lord Macaulay*, i. 67 note (1876).
[3] *Force of Truth*, pp. 17–18 (R.T.S.).

delusions."[1] The victory rested, however, entirely with Newton Scott's unorthodox opinions vanished, and for the rest of hi life he was an earnest Evangelical. It was during his ministr in London that he wrote his *Commentary on the Bible,* whic was for so many years so famous. Carefully avoiding all force or fanciful interpretations, he wrote in a common-sense styl with the aim of speaking plainly to persons of ordinary capacity Its immediate success was very great, and Scott's *Commentar* was soon found in almost every Evangelical home. Cardina Newman states that Scott was "the writer who made a deepe impression on my mind than any other, and to whom (humanly speaking) I almost owe my soul."[2]

In the country there were an increasing number of clergy holding Evangelical views, and doing earnest and useful work usually started in the face of strong opposition, which graduall gave way before a faithful and devoted ministry. Among these were Vincent Perronet, Vicar of Shoreham, Robinson of Leicester, Stillingfleet of Hotham, the learned Thomas Clarke of Chesham Bois in Buckinghamshire, Richardson of York, and Joseph Milner of Hull (brother of Isaac Milner), who deserves special notice on account of the fame he acquired as the author of *The History of the Church of Christ.* This work easily took a first place amongst Evangelical literature. Milner's avowed object was to emphasise the great blessings which had resulted from the spread of Christianity, and he avoided as far as possible any mention of the abuses and heresies which had too often hindered its progress. He desired to write a record of the genuine piety which had been displayed by the real followers of Christ in all ages. It soon became very popular, especially amongst Evangelicals, because Milner gave great, and many have thought undue, prominence to the lives of those Christians who in every age, from the time of the Apostles right down to the Reformation, held Evangelical doctrines.

The name of Dr. Samuel Johnson (1709–84), the staunch Churchman and celebrated lexicographer, may perhaps be fittingly introduced here. Although in his earlier years he had, as a typical eighteenth-century Churchman, strongly condemned Methodist "enthusiasm," towards the end of his life he seems to have possessed decided Evangelical leanings. Cowper rejoiced at the account which Newton gave him of the spiritual change which

[1] *Force of Truth,* pp. 17–18 (R.T.S.).
[2] *Apologia,* ch. i. p. 3.

ad passed over Dr. Johnson, and in an epitaph described him s a man

> "Who many a noble gift from Heaven possessed,
> And faith at last—alone worth all the rest."[1]

His lifelong fear of death seems to have been overcome, and his dying testimony was, "I offer up my soul to the great and merciful God. I offer it full of pollution, but in the full assurance that it will be cleansed in the blood of the Redeemer."[2]

Throughout his whole life his robust and sterling Christianity had exerted a wide and powerful influence for good. "There must," said Johnson, in talking of religion, "be either a natural or moral stupidity, if one lives in a total neglect of so very important a concern."[3] Thackeray declared that "Johnson was revered as a sort of oracle . . . and that his immense authority reconciled the nation to loyalty, and shamed it out of irreligion."[4]

CHAPTER XI

RESULTS OF THE EVANGELICAL REVIVAL

(a) *The "Clapham Sect" and its Work*

THE great religious and social movements for the benefit of humanity which were set on foot at the close of the eighteenth century were convincing evidence of the fact that Evangelicalism did not consist merely in the enthusiastic propagation of a barren theological creed, however orthodox, but was a healthy branch of that "good tree which is known by its fruit." "Both the onslaught upon the slave trade," says an eminent authority, "and the other remarkable philanthropic efforts towards the last quarter of the last century arose in, and owed their importance to, the great Evangelical movement."[5]

[1] *Cowper's Letters*, p. 192.
[2] W. Roberts, *Life and Correspondence of Mrs. Hannah More*, i. 393 (1834).
[3] Boswell's *Life of Johnson*, vol. ii. p. 466.
[4] Quoted in Overton and Relton, p. 285.
[5] Lord Morley in *Nineteenth Century*, Feb. 1892.

The little suburban village (as it then was) of Clapham will always be largely associated with these beneficent results of the Evangelical revival, because the great work which was either achieved or undertaken during these years was to a large extent due to the initiation, persistent devotion, and noble self-sacrifice of a small but exceedingly influential group of laymen who resided there, and who were soon popularly styled the "Clapham Sect." They were all staunch members of the National Church, and derived the inspiration for their work from their strong Evangelical principles, which were zealously stimulated under the faithful ministry of John Venn, the Rector of Clapham 1792–1813, a worthy son of Henry Venn, a former curate of the parish. The early sneer at "Methodist" preaching for attracting only the low-born and ignorant had lost its force when John Venn numbered amongst his regular hearers such prominent men as Charles Grant, the Chairman of the East India Company; Zachary Macaulay, a former Governor of Sierra Leone; Lord Teignmouth, a former Governor-General of India; Henry Thornton, the wealthy banker and merchant; James Stephen, the eminent lawyer; and, above all, William Wilberforce, the Court favourite, the friend of Pitt and the famous Parliamentary orator.

The time and energies of these men were whole-heartedly devoted to all work which had for its object the improvement and amelioration of the lot of the poor and down-trodden. Church-building, the establishment of day schools and savings banks, and the reform of the disgraceful condition of and discipline prevailing in prisons, all claimed their earnest attention. Probably no better example can be found of the right appreciation of the responsibilities connected with great riches than the lives of John Thornton (1720–90) and his son Henry (1760–1815). Both these large-hearted men regarded themselves literally as stewards of the wealth they possessed. John Thornton's purse was always open to supply the needs of every good cause. He distributed Bibles and Prayer Books and Christian literature in all parts of the world where English-speaking people were found. He purchased advowsons in order to fill them with earnest and active incumbents, and he regularly assisted the Evangelical clergy with money for charitable purposes. Daniel Rowlands had permission to draw on him whenever he pleased, and John Newton received a regular allowance of £200 a year. His son Henry inherited to the full his father's generosity. It is estimated that as a bachelor he regularly gave away six-sevenths of his income.

and even after his marriage he spent only one-third on himself and his family.

But the most celebrated name in connection with the Clapham Sect will always be that of William Wilberforce (1759–1831). Although in his earlier years he seems to have indulged for a time in the dissipations of a fashionable life, yet it would appear that he was always of a sober and serious disposition. On the first night of his arrival at Cambridge, he says, "I was introduced to as licentious a set of men as can well be conceived. They drank hard, and their conversation was even worse than their lives. I lived amongst them for some time, though I never relished their society; often indeed I was horror-struck at their conduct, and after the first year I shook off my connection with them."[1] When he was twenty-five years of age he passed through a gradual but very real spiritual experience. "By degrees," he says, "the promises and offers of the Gospel produced in me something of a settled peace of conscience. I devoted myself, for whatever might be the term of my future life, to the service of my God and Saviour, and, with many infirmities and deficiencies, through His help I continue to this day."[2]

He soon threw himself vigorously into religious and social work, forming societies to restrain vice and immorality, especially amongst the upper classes, and "for the better observance of the Sabbath day." He endeavoured to advance the Evangelical cause by obtaining an influence over Church patronage and by promoting the establishment of the *Christian Observer*; but the publication of his powerful treatise, *A Practical View of the prevailing Religious System of Professed Christians in the Higher and Middle Classes in this Country contrasted with real Christianity*, was the most convincing proof of his Evangelical sympathies. It was exceedingly popular, and had a wide and rapid circulation, 7500 copies being sold in six months, and it was soon translated into five different languages. His aim, as the long title of the book implies, was to expose the formal and defective religion then professed and to show, from the transforming effect of his own conversion, that Christianity was not the mere system of ethics which had become popular as a reaction against the strictness of Puritan theology.

But Wilberforce's fame will always justly rest on the all-important part he played in the Abolition of the Slave Trade.

[1] *Life of Wilberforce*, by his sons, vol. i. p. 10 (1838).
[2] Ibid., p. 112.

It is happily almost impossible to realise in the present day the magnitude of the task which confronted him and his faithful "Clapham" supporters, Thomas Clarkson, Zachary Macaulay, and James Stephen, in their efforts to arouse public feeling on this question; for although they received the sympathy and support of Granville Sharp, Pitt, Burke, Bishops Porteus and Watson, yet the "Clapham Sect" was the real mainspring of the movement.[1] It is simply astounding to think of the apathy and open opposition of even definitely Christian people to this humane design. We can form some idea of the tremendous task which Wilberforce and his friends had undertaken when we learn that even Whitefield defended the practice of slavery on the ground that there were slaves in Abraham's household.[2] A vast amount of English capital was invested in the trade, and the custom had been so long established that it was a thoroughly recognised institution, and most people were fully persuaded that any attempt to overturn it would seriously imperil the safety of our West Indian possessions. Numberless meetings were held and a vast amount of literature circulated to expose the horrors and barbarous cruelties of this degrading traffic in human lives, and the eloquent pen of the Evangelical poet was freely used on behalf of the poor, suffering negroes.

"Forced from home and all its pleasures,
Afric's coast I left forlorn;
To increase a stranger's treasures,
O'er the raging billows borne.
Men from England bought and sold me;
Paid my price in paltry gold;
But, though slave they have enrolled me,
Minds are never to be sold.

Still in thought as free as ever,
What are England's rights, I ask,
Me from my delights to sever,
Me to torture, me to task?
Fleecy locks and black complexion
Cannot forfeit nature's claim,
Skins may differ, but affection
Dwells in white and black the same.

[1] The Quakers also actively supported the movement, and they had been the first body of Christians which officially condemned the Slave Trade.

[2] *Cf.* Andrews, *Life of Whitefield*, pp. 206–7.

Is there, as ye sometimes tell us,
Is there One who reigns on high?
Has He bid you buy and sell us;
Speaking from His throne the sky?
Ask Him, if your knotted scourges,
Matches, blood extorting screws,
Are the means that duty urges
Agents of His Will to use?"[1]

Again and again Wilberforce and his party were defeated in the House of Commons, but there was no thought of giving up the struggle. "I could not sleep," he wrote, "the poor blacks rushed into my mind, and the guilt of our wicked land."[2]

At length after a strenuous crusade, lasting twenty years, the violent opposition was overcome, and in 1807 the Slave Trade was declared illegal by Parliament, although slavery itself was not abolished till 1833.

The name of Hannah More (1745–1833), although she lived and worked far away from Clapham, must be mentioned in connection with the Evangelical circle there, on account of her close association with some of its leading members. Originally moving in a fashionable and literary circle, she was, and always remained, the intimate friend of Sir Joshua Reynolds, Garrick, Horace Walpole, and Dr. Johnson. From 1781 she came into contact with John Newton, through whose preaching and influence she was brought into close sympathy with Evangelicalism, while her future work led her into friendly association with Bishop Porteus, Thornton, and Wilberforce. Her wide circle of friendship enabled her to exercise a powerful influence beyond the scope of the ordinary Evangelical. "You have a great advantage, madam," wrote Newton to her; "there is a circle by which what you write will be read, and which will hardly read anything of a religious kind that is not written by you."[3]

Her writings were very numerous and exceedingly popular. *Thoughts on the Manners of the Great* (1788) exerted a wide and very salutary influence on the lives of the upper classes, while her *Village Politics* and *Cheap Repository Tracts*, published at the time of the French Revolution to influence the opinions of the lower classes, certainly contributed in no small measure to prevent the spread of revolutionary theories in England, and

[1] Cowper's *The Negro's Complaint.*
[2] *Cf.* Stock, *One Hundred Years of C.M.S.*, p. 21.
[3] *Life and Correspondence of Mrs. Hannah More*, ii. 265.

were a powerful antidote to the sceptical and infidel literature which was being so widely circulated at the time by the disciples of the author of the *Rights of Man*.

But her energies were by no means confined to the publication of religious and wholesome literature. The deplorable condition of the neighbourhood where she resided soon led her to attempt some practical measures of reform. The terrible poverty and wickedness, the appalling moral and spiritual depravity which prevailed amongst the people, impelled her to commence a system of regular secular and religious instruction for the children and adults of the district. "We saw," she writes, "but one Bible in the parish of Cheddar, and that was used to prop up a flower-pot." [1] The vicar lived at Oxford, and thirteen of the surrounding parishes were without a resident curate, and the only incumbent living in the neighbourhood was reported "to be intoxicated about six times a week, and frequently prevented from preaching by two black eyes honestly earned by fighting." [2]

The difficulties and opposition she encountered in her task of establishing day and Sunday schools seem incredible. Parents were afraid lest their children should become so under the power of Hannah More that they might be sold as slaves! Land-owners feared that religion would make the poor lazy and useless, and farmers objected to their labourers being educated. She was described as a "Methodist" and even a "revolutionary," while one officious curate actually succeeded in interrupting her work at a certain village for a time; but with persevering efforts and the financial support of Thornton and Wilberforce all these obstacles were surmounted, and the schools and religious instruction proved an incalculable blessing to the neighbourhood. Bibles were distributed, and numbers were taught to read and work, and many were reclaimed from lives of vice, drunkenness, or degradation. These voluntary and self-denying labours also reproved the clergy for their culpable laxity and neglect of duty, and stimulated them to endeavour to redeem their lost reputation.

It is well here to mention the origin of the organisation for definite weekly religious instruction of the young, which was formed at this time, and which has long since been adopted in all parts of the Christian world. Sunday schools were not entirely unknown, as they had been started in Milan in the seventeenth century, and there had been isolated schools in England before

[1] Green (*ante*), p. 717.

[2] *Life and Correspondence of Mrs. Hannah More*, ii. 209.

this time, but it was due to the experiment made by Robert Raikes (1735–1811), an Evangelical layman and a friend of Wesley and Whitefield, that they first became a regularly organised branch of parochial work. It was in 1780 that Raikes, scandalised at the wretched and almost heathenish condition of some of the poor children playing in the streets of Gloucester, "made an agreement with four decent and well-disposed women to receive as many children as he should send upon the Sunday, whom they were to instruct in reading and in the Church Catechism,"[1] enlisting at the same time the services of the curate of the parish to visit them regularly and note their progress. The task of training and taming these wild young spirits was by no means easy, but the success of the experiment was soon proved by the fact that after a few years it was no uncommon sight to see Raikes voluntarily accompanied by quite a number of these little ill-clad "scholars" as he attended the daily Cathedral service.[2]

In 1783 he published an account of his organisation which attracted very general attention, and similar attempts were soon made in other places, the Evangelical clergy especially warmly adopting the Sunday-school system. As early as 1784 John Wesley states: "I find these schools springing up wherever I go. Perhaps God may have a deeper end therein than men are aware of. Who knows but some of these schools may become nurseries for Christians?"[3] The methods were, however, different from those employed to-day, as it was necessary first to teach the children to read and write before they could be given satisfactory religious instruction, and the teachers for a time were usually paid a small fee. A large amount of ignorance and prejudice also had to be overcome, as a leading bishop actually declared that there was "much ground for suspicion that sedition and atheism were the real objects of some of these institutions rather than religion."[4]

(*b*) *The Religious Societies and Missionary Enterprise*

It has been well remarked "that there was hardly a single missionary or philanthropic scheme of the day which was not either originated or warmly taken up by the Evangelical party."[5]

[1] Letter in *Gentleman's Magazine*, June 1784, p. 411.
[2] *Cf.* Balleine (*ante*), p. 140. [3] *Journal*, July 18, 1784.
[4] Quoted in Overton and Relton (*ante*), p. 304.
[5] *Eng. Ch. in 18th Cent.*, p. 315.

Thus all the great religious and missionary societies which were formed at the close of the eighteenth century were due to the efforts of men of Evangelical sympathies, the members of the Clapham Sect playing a prominent part.

Very few attempts had been made during the century towards the evangelisation of the heathen ; the Church itself had no definite organisation for carrying the Gospel to pagan countries. The Society for promoting Christian Knowledge had, it is true, subsidised the efforts of Lutheran missionaries in India, but this was beyond the scope of its recognised work, while the labours of the Society for the Propagation of the Gospel were strictly limited by its charter to the British dominions. It had been established to support clergy in the Colonies, and thus " only indirectly and accidently touched the heathen." " Both these two venerable institutions only recognised the duty of the Church to the heathen in an indirect and imperfect manner." [1] There was therefore abundant need for direct missionary effort to be undertaken. In 1792 the **Baptist Missionary Society** was formed, and William Carey went out to work amongst the natives of India. In September 1795, largely owing to an appeal made in the *Evangelical Magazine*, it was resolved to form " an extensive and regularly organised (Missionary) Society, to consist of Evangelical and lay brethren of all denominations." This organisation, afterwards styled the **London Missionary Society,** formed a committee consisting of two Churchmen, two ministers of the Established Church of Scotland, two Methodists, three Independents, and one English Presbyterian. In 1796 it commenced work amongst the South Sea Islands. [2]

But the practical difficulties in connection with the establishment and development of native churches, arising from the want of a definite ecclesiastical basis in this new organisation, inclined Churchmen to view it with dissatisfaction, and gradually led to their withdrawal from its ranks and their earnest desire for the formation of a Society conducted on exclusively Church lines. As far back as 1786 a discussion had taken place in the " Eclectic Society," composed mainly of Evangelical clergy, on the question, " What is the best method of planting and propagating the Gospel in Botany Bay ? " In 1793 Wilberforce had endeavoured to get the East India Company to attempt some missionary work in India, and had obtained the insertion of a clause in the India Bill

[1] Perry, *Ch. Hist.*, vol. iii. p. 538.
[2] *Cf.* Stoughton (*ante*), vol. ii. p. 336.

pledging the Company "to seek the religious and moral improvement of the native inhabitants of the British dominions in India." The opposition of the Company, however, rendered this clause a dead letter, and Wilberforce became a strong advocate for the formation of an independent Church Society to undertake missionary work in the East.

About the same time a sum of £4000 had been left to a leading Evangelical clergyman to be spent "for the best advantage of the interests of religion." The Eclectic Society decided that this money could not be better employed than in sending out messengers of the Gospel to the heathen, and at a meeting of the same Society in March 1799, Charles Simeon proposed the three questions "What can we do?" "When shall we do it?" and "How shall we do it?" It was felt impossible to join the London Missionary Society, and it was therefore decided to form a fresh Society at once and to lay the plans before the heads of the Church.[1] Thus on April 12 a meeting was held at the Castle and Falcon Inn, Aldersgate Street, "for the purpose of instituting a Society amongst members of the Established Church for sending missionaries among the heathen." "A Society for Missions to Africa and the East" was formed, with Henry Venn as Chairman, Thornton as Treasurer, and Scott as Secretary. Sixteen clergymen and nine laymen pledged themselves to promote the new enterprise. The infant Society received very material aid from the Clapham friends, Thornton, Zachary Macaulay, J. Stephen, Granville Sharp, and Charles Grant being among its most enthusiastic supporters. Josiah Pratt succeeded Scott as Secretary in 1802, and in 1812 the name was changed to the now familiar title of the **Church Missionary Society.**

It encountered great difficulties at first from a lack of men willing to undertake the novel and perilous task of evangelising the heathen, and after waiting three years the Society was reluctantly obliged to employ some German Lutherans, and the first mission was started in Sierra Leone, where Henry Thornton had formed a company establishing a colony for liberated slaves. The story of the Society's marvellous growth in the next century, until at length its missionary stations circled the whole globe, lies beyond the scope of this little volume.

Besides the valuable work done by the Society for the Promotion of Christian Knowledge in the circulation of religious books and tracts, and the establishment of parochial libraries in

[1] *Cf.* Carus, *Life of Simeon*, pp. 125–6.

England and America, several other attempts on a smaller scale had been made for the promotion of Christian Truth by similar methods. In 1750 an undenominational "Society for Diffusing Religious Knowledge among the Poor" had been formed, and John Wesley had also circulated a large number of tracts in connection with his evangelistic labours.[1]

The distribution of tracts dealing with the current vices of the times had formed part of the work of the "Society for the Reformation of Manners," started by Wilberforce in 1787, while Hannah More had rendered valuable service to the cause of religion by the circulation of her "Cheap Repository Tracts" (3 a month). But the same year that witnessed the founding of the Church Missionary Society saw also the formation of the **Religious Tract Society.** It was largely due to the efforts of the Rev. George Burder of Coventry, and was designed to be of a more comprehensive and permanent character than these smaller undertakings, while it differed from the S.P.C.K. in not being founded on a strictly Church basis. It was felt that in the circulation of religious and wholesome literature the united action of members of different religious communions would accentuate the essential oneness in the spiritual aims and purpose of all true Christians, without compromising any special ecclesiastical principle or endangering any distinctive denominational interest. Thus the supporters of the Religious Tract Society included a number of prominent Dissenters as well as such Churchmen as Rowland Hill, the famous evangelist, Edward Bickersteth, William Goode, Legh Richmond, and Zachary Macaulay. The sale of its tracts, published at the lowest prices, soon numbered over a million a year.

The British and Foreign Bible Society, although not actually organised till the early years of the next century, was really a product of the Evangelical Revival. The circumstances which in a large measure led to its formation are almost romantic. The Revival had produced a marked spiritual effect in Wales, and had led to a far more general desire for the study of the Scriptures by the Welsh people. Unfortunately, however, there was a general scarcity of Welsh Bibles, the Society for Promoting Christian Knowledge not having issued a single copy for thirty years until 1799, when 10,000 were printed, a number which proved totally inadequate to meet the demand. An urgent application for this edition had been made in 1792, but the Society

[1] Cf. *Journal,* Dec. 18, 1745.

had declined to grant it, on the ground that it was not required. When the edition at length appeared in 1799 it was found "insufficient to supply one-fourth part of the country." "The joy of those," says a contemporary, "who received the Bibles amounted to exultation; and the grief of those who could not obtain a copy fell little short of anguish."[1]

In 1800 a little Welsh peasant girl, who had been hoarding her small earnings for the past six years in order to possess a Bible of her own, walked fifty miles to Bala to purchase a copy of the Scriptures from the celebrated Welsh Evangelist Thomas Charles, only to learn that the last available Bible had just been sold. This pathetic incident, illustrating the pressing need of a further supply of the Scriptures, determined Charles to use every effort to satisfy the spiritual wants of his countrymen. The S.P.C.K. were again approached, but refused for the time to give any further help. "I have repeatedly tried the Society for Promoting Christian Knowledge through the medium of my friends, men of influence," wrote the Rev. T. Jones of Creaton, in June 1802, "and found that no further help can be expected from them now; they gave a decided answer *more than twice over*."[1] Thus in 1802 Charles propounded to the Committee of the Religious Tract Society the idea of the formation of a Society with the sole object of publishing and distributing the Scriptures. The scheme was warmly taken up, one member exclaiming: "Surely a Society might be formed for the purpose, and if for Wales, why not for the world?"[2]

Two years later the British and Foreign Bible Society was started, on the same inter-denominational basis as the Religious Tract Society, to circulate copies of the Word of God "without note or comment," with the proviso that one of the Secretaries must be a clergyman of the Established Church and the other a Nonconformist minister. It was actively supported by Granville Sharp, Bishop Porteus, and two of the Welsh bishops, while Lord Teignmouth was the first President, Wilberforce Vice-President, Thornton Treasurer, and Josiah Pratt one of the Secretaries. Its first work was to bring out an edition of the Welsh Bible for the use of Sunday-schools in the Principality.

[1] Morgan, *Life of T. Charles*, p. 285 (1828).
[2] Cf. *The Story of Mary Jones and her Bible*, p. 110.

CHAPTER XII

RELATIONS WITH COLONIAL AND FOREIGN CHURCHES

After the formation of the "Society for the Propagation of the Gospel in Foreign Parts" in 1701, regular and systematic Church work was commenced amongst the rapidly increasing English colonists in North America. The difficulties connected with the work were, however, considerable. In the most important provinces the inhabitants were either quite out of sympathy with, or openly antagonistic to, the Episcopal system. In the New England States Puritan Independency was virtually established, while Pennsylvania was strongly Quaker and Maryland was Roman Catholic. In the other provinces religion seems too often to have been almost entirely neglected, large numbers of the settlers living openly sinful and godless lives. One of the S.P.G. missionaries describes the inhabitants of South Carolina as "the vilest race of men upon the earth; they have neither honour or honesty, nor religion enough to entitle them to any tolerable character, being a perfect medley or hotchpotch of bankrupts, pirates, decayed libertines, sectaries, and enthusiasts of all sorts."[1] Archbishop Secker also confirmed this sad account when he said that "too many of the first European inhabitants (of the Southern States) carried but little sense of Christianity abroad with them. A great part of the rest suffered it to wear out gradually, and their children grew, of course, to have yet less than they, till in some countries there were scarce any footsteps of it left beyond the mere name."[2]

Naturally the work of the Society was grievously hindered during the period of the War of Independence, and at its close it was obliged to withdraw altogether. The clergy frequently suffered great hardships and privations, and were often compelled to discontinue their ministrations, as the people generally suspected them of espousing the British side in the struggle, and strongly objected to the prayers in the Liturgy for the Royal Family. At the conclusion of the war many of the S.P.G. clergy migrated to New Brunswick or Nova Scotia.

[1] Hawkins, *Historical Notices*, p. 54 (1845).
[2] Southey, *Life of Wesley*, p. 296.

Another hindrance to effective Church work in the Colonies at this time was the great difficulty experienced in finding suitable men to labour amongst the people, as the spiritual character of the Colonial clergy, with some brilliant exceptions, seems to have been far from satisfactory. The preacher of the anniversary sermon for the S.P.G. stated, in 1716, "that the two great difficulties that still lie hard upon our Society are the want of sober and religious missionaries, few offering themselves to that service for the glory of God and the good of souls, but chiefly to find a refuge from poverty and scandal."[1] John Wesley, on the other hand, records that he had heard at a visitation of clergy of South Carolina "such a conversation on Christ Our Righteousness as he had not heard at any visitation in England,"[2] and Bishop Berkeley specially commends the character of the S.P.G. missionaries in the New England provinces. Thus Archbishop Secker's wholesale condemnation of them as "men of desperate fortunes, low qualifications, and bad and doubtful characters,"[3] would seem to be too severe; especially when we bear in mind that when the S.P.G. commenced its work in America only five churches existed, but that when it was obliged to retire, owing to the Rebellion, it left two hundred and fifty fully established congregations.

In spite of all these difficulties and disadvantages, a large amount of good work was accomplished amongst the white, black, and Indian inhabitants. The Rev. George Keith, who went out to New England at the beginning of the century, was successful in forming a large number of churches and congregations. Wesley and Whitefield laboured faithfully in the newly formed Colony of Georgia, although the latter's zeal as an itinerating evangelist militated against his usefulness in building up the Church in any one district or locality. In North Carolina the labours of Clement Hall were quite apostolic. Besides acting as missionary to the Indians in the neighbourhood, he was most earnest and active in his work amongst the colonists. Large crowds gathered to hear him wherever he preached, and in eight years (1743–51) he journeyed 14,000 miles, preached 675 sermons, and baptised 3783 white and 243 black children, 57 white adults and 112 black.

The self-denying efforts of the accomplished and scholarly Bishop Berkeley to found a Training College in Bermuda for

[1] *Life of Bp. Kennet*, p. 123 (1730). [2] *Journal*, April 22, 1737.
[3] Letter to H. Walpole in Secker's *Sermons*, p. 344, edn. 1780.

candidates for the colonial ministry and for workers amongst the Indians, must not be overlooked. Entirely owing to his eloquent and persuasive appeals, he collected in England some £5000, and succeeded in overcoming the prejudice of the Government to his University scheme, and in 1726 he obtained a Royal Charter and a grant of £20,000 towards the proposed college. He went out to Rhode Island with three other fellows of Trinity College, Dublin, in 1728, in order to take up his new duties as President of the Bermuda Academy; but owing to the faithlessness of the English Government the promised grant was never paid, and he was obliged to return to England, without accomplishing anything, in 1731.[1]

Missionary work amongst the negroes and Indians was attended with exceptional difficulties, owing to the indifferent and hostile attitude adopted towards them by so many of the colonists, and especially the slave-owners, who usually regarded them rather as beasts of burden than as human beings capable of moral and spiritual enlightenment. Berkeley alludes to the "ancient apathy" of the first planters "to the Indians," and "to an irrational contempt for the blacks as creatures of another species who had no right to be instructed," as proving "a main obstacle to the conversion of these poor people."[2]

But notwithstanding the difficulties and discouragements, numerous conversions resulted from the evangelistic labours amongst both negroes and Indians, and there is the record of a somewhat pathetic request of some Iroquois chiefs in the neighbourhood of Albany to Queen Anne, in 1703, "who hoped she would be a good mother, and send them some one to teach them religion as well as traffic."[3]

Probably the greatest hindrance to the development and extension of Church work in the colonies was the crying need of an American Episcopate. With the clergy and people of the entire continent under the supervision of the Bishop of London, it was impossible for the Church system of government or discipline to be effectively carried out. Confirmations were necessarily unknown, and no real control or guidance could be exercised over the clergy, while candidates for the ministry had to travel at least three thousand miles to receive ordination. Bishop Sherlock writes in 1752: "I think myself in a very bad situation, Bishop of a vast country, without power or influence,

[1] *Cf.* Anderson's *Hist. of Colonial Church*, vol. iii. p. 366 (1856).
[2] Ibid., vol. iii. pp. 376 and 433. [3] Ibid., vol. iii. p. 584.

or any means of promoting true religion, sequestered from a people over whom I have the care and must never hope to see." [1]

Strenuous efforts had been made at different times by influential Churchmen, all through the century, to remedy this glaring defect,[2] but the English Government, if not openly hostile, was at least apathetic in the matter, and feared giving offence to the Dissenters at home, and especially to those in the colonies, who dreaded lest the colonial bishops should arrogate to themselves a temporal and persecuting power, which had rendered the Episcopal order so obnoxious to their Puritan forefathers. Frequent and earnest requests were, however, received from colonial Churchmen on the subject. In 1724 Samuel Johnson, a prominent S.P.G. missionary in Connecticut, wrote to the Bishop of London, telling him that "the fountain of all our misery is the want of a bishop, for whom there are many thousands of souls in this country who do impatiently long and pray, and for want of do extremely suffer." [3]

On the recognition of the independence of the United States the matter was taken up in earnest, and in 1784, as the Archbishop of Canterbury felt unable to assist, Samuel Seabury obtained consecration from some Scottish Episcopal bishops as Bishop of Connecticut. In 1785 the General Convention of the clergy and laity adhering to the Episcopal system in America officially requested the Archbishop of Canterbury to set apart the divines they selected as bishops of the "Protestant Episcopal Church" in America. After a special Act of Parliament had been obtained to render this proceeding legal, William White and Samuel Provoost were consecrated, in February 1787, to the sees of Pennsylvania and New York. In the same year the foundation of a regularly organised Colonial Church was laid by the consecration of Dr. Charles Inglis, formerly rector of Trinity Church, New York, as first Bishop of Nova Scotia, and in 1793 the see of Quebec was formed.

In 1717 an interesting correspondence took place between Archbishop Wake and some of the leading doctors of the Sorbonne in Paris, with a view to a *rapprochement* between the English and Gallican Churches. It was occasioned by the autocratic

[1] Chandler's *Life of Dr. S. Johnson*, p. 133 (1805).

[2] Archbishop Secker, writing on the subject in 1751, stated: "I believe there scarce is or ever was a bishop in the Church of England, from the Revolution to this day, that hath not desired the establishment of bishops in our Colonies." (Letter to H. Walpole in *Sermons*, p. 348, edn. 1780.)

[3] Quoted in Overton and Relton, p. 328.

action of the Papal Court in publishing the bull *Unigenitus* in 1713, which was directly levelled at the Jansenists and the cherished liberties of the Gallican Church. Several leading French Churchmen urged the right of appeal from the Pope to a General Council, and de Gerardin and the celebrated ecclesiastical historian Du Pin expressed a desire for union with the Church of England; Du Pin remarked that "the differences between them, on most points, was not so great as to render a reconciliation impracticable, and that it was his earnest wish that all Christians should be united in one sheepfold."

Wake entered heartily into the proposal, and dwelt on the purity of the Anglican Church in doctrine and discipline, and insisted on the renunciation of the Pope's supremacy as essential to any real success of the project, emphasising the principle laid down in Article XXXIV. of the independence (as to all matters of authority) of every national Church of all others. As regards "points of doctrine," he urged that they should endeavour "to agree as far as possible in all articles of any moment, and for other matters to allow a difference 'till God shall bring us to a union in these also.'" He stoutly contended that any negotiation must be conducted on an equal footing between the two churches. "I am a friend to peace but more to truth. They may depend on it," he wrote to Mr. Beauvoir, the English chaplain in Paris, "I shall always account our Church to stand upon an equal foot with theirs . . . the Church of England is free, is orthodox. She has a plenary authority within herself, and has not need to recur to any other church to direct her what to retain, or what to do." [1]

Owing to the interference and bitter hostility of the Jesuits the correspondence came to nothing, and Archbishop Wake only incurred the suspicion of endangering the Protestant position of the Church by his efforts. It is not surprising that Wake's intentions should have been misunderstood, when we remember the uncompromising hostility towards Rome which had been displayed by almost all Churchmen since the Reformation, and was "one of the most strongly marked features in the Churchmanship of the time," [2] of which the disgraceful "Gordon Riots" in 1780 were a painful illustration.

It is abundantly clear, however, that Wake's action was due

[1] Mosheim's *Eccles. Hist.* (Maclaine), vol. vi. pp. 70, 99, 102, and 111. Appen. III., Letters Nos. iii., iv., and viii. (edn. 1810).

[2] *Eng. Ch. in 18th Cent.*, p. 148.

entirely to his liberal and catholic spirit and the earnest desire he possessed to reunite, as far as possible, divided Christendom. Thus in 1719 he professed the most cordial friendship towards the Foreign Reformed Churches. "Although he wished they had a moderate Episcopal government, yet he would welcome a closer union amongst all the Reformed bodies at almost any price";[1] and in 1724 he wrote to Father Courayer: "I bless God I was born and bred in an Episcopal Church, which, I am convinced, has been the government established in the Christian Church from the very time of the Apostles. But I should be unwilling to affirm, that where the ministry is not episcopal there is no Church, nor any true administration of the sacraments. And very many there are among us who are zealous for Episcopacy, and yet dare not go so far as to annul the ordinances of God performed by any other ministry."[2]

An attempt at reunion of a different character had been tentatively made a few years previously, when Frederick I. of Prussia attempted to introduce Episcopacy into the Lutheran Church in his dominions. He had conferred the title of bishop on two of his clergy in 1700, and desired them to endeavour to reunite the Lutheran and Reformed communions on a mutual episcopal basis similar to that of the English Church. In 1706 negotiations were opened with the Archbishop of Canterbury, and the English Liturgy was translated into German and introduced into the King's Chapel. Archbishop Sharp, whose affection for foreign Protestants was so cordial that he declared that "he would communicate with the foreign Reformed Churches wherever he might chance to be abroad,"[3] warmly supported the proposal, while Queen Anne and Bishop Smalridge were also strongly in sympathy with the movement. There was, however, a fear that the Thirty-nine Articles would savour of a "little too much Geneva stamp" in Berlin, and the conferences languished, and on the death of the King in 1713 ceased altogether.[4]

The relations between the Church of England and the Moravian Brethren during this century have a special interest at the present time, in view of the suggestions towards reunion made at recent Lambeth Conferences. In 1715, on the representation of Archbishop Wake, a Royal *Brief* was granted, ordering

[1] *Mosheim* (Maclaine), vi, 124, Letter No. xix.
[2] *Mosheim* (by Murdock), p. 873, note 1.
[3] *Life*, by his son, ii. 28 (1825).
[4] Cf. *Life of Arch. Sharp*, ed. Newcombe, i. 410–49 (1825).

collections to be made in churches for "the relief and for the preserving of the Episcopal Churches in Great Poland and Polish Prussia." A correspondence ensued between Wake and the Moravian bishop, Jablonsky, with the result that the English bishops warmly advocated the needs of the Moravian Church. Again in 1737, on the consecration of Count Zinzendorf as a Moravian bishop, Archbishop Potter sent a letter of congratulation and greeting, in which he professed himself ever ready "especially to love and embrace your Church, united with us in the closest bonds of love, and which has hitherto, as we have been informed, invariably maintained both the purest primitive faith and the discipline of the primitive Church." [1] On another occasion Archbishop Potter declared that "he had been led to the conviction that the Church of the Brethren is truly an apostolic and episcopal Church, whose doctrines contain nothing whatever militating against the Thirty-nine Articles of the Church of England." [2] This view was confirmed a little later, when a Bill which was passed in 1749, to encourage the Moravians to settle in the colonies, acknowledged the "Unitas Fratrum" or "United Brethren" to be "an ancient Protestant Episcopal Church," and declared "their doctrine to differ in no essential article of faith from the Church of England." [2] It was in this year also that Bishop Wilson of Sodor and Man accepted the invitation of the Moravian Synod in London to act as superintendent over the Brethren. [3]

CHAPTER XIII

NONJURORS AND NONCONFORMISTS

It may be well here to give a short account of two very divergent channels of religious life and thought, both of which existed outside the National Church, their mutual estrangement from which was, however, almost their only common bond. The Nonjurors schism had been started owing to the dynastic change involved in the Revolution of 1689. The separation from the Church, on

[1] Doddridge's *Corres.*, iii. 264.
[2] *Memoirs of James Hutton*, by Benham, p. 24 (1856).
[3] Hutton, *Short History of Moravian Church*, pp. 211–12 (1895).

a question mainly technical, of a considerable body of learned and eminently pious men, thoroughly in sympathy with her doctrines, was a very serious loss, especially during the earlier years of the century, when among the Nonjurors were such celebrated names as Bishop Ken, Dean Hickes, Robert Nelson, and Henry Dodwell. In their doctrinal and ecclesiastical views they were all high Churchmen, but their intense hatred towards the Established Church and all who had, by complying with the existing government, repudiated the "doctrine of the Cross," as they styled the tenet of "Non-Resistance," severed them completely from the sympathy and fellowship of their High Church brethren within "the pale." Thus it was only to the persecuted and struggling Scottish Episcopal Church, so closely akin to them in its political and ecclesiastical views, that they were able to turn for friendship and communion.

This peculiar isolation of their position, combined with their narrow and exclusive ecclesiastical theories, led them before long into the troubled pathway of internal strife and divisions. In 1718 a dispute arose over the use of the Liturgy, which led to a division of their forces into two hostile camps. The "*Usagers*," as they were styled, led by Bishops Collier and Brett, refused to use the Book of Common Prayer, substituting in its stead a new liturgy and Communion Office, mainly based on King Edward VI.'s First Prayer Book; while the "Regular" body, supported by Spinkes and Leslie, remained firm in their allegiance to the authorised "use" of the Church of England. Later on in the century further divisions occurred over the question of lay baptism. Episcopal consecrations were maintained by the opposing parties, the last bishop of the "Regular" line dying in 1779, and the last of the "Irregulars" in 1805.

Although the Nonjurors, fully sharing the staunch and often intolerant Protestantism of the times, were strongly averse to any idea of reunion with Rome, yet in 1717 they enthusiastically entered into negotiations with the Orthodox Eastern Church with a view to a union. They offered to make very liberal concessions in order to arrive at a concordat, but they took exception to the decrees of Councils being placed on the same level as Holy Scripture, to any direct worship of the Virgin Mary, to the invocation of Saints, the doctrine of Transubstantiation, and the worshipping by pictures. The Eastern Church, however, remained obstinately obdurate on all these points, simply informing them that "they must submit to them with sincerity and obedience and without any scruple or dispute,"[1] and thus the attempt came to nothing.

By far the most famous of the later Nonjurors was William Law (1686–1761). Refusing to take the oaths on the accession of George I., he resigned his Fellowship at Cambridge, and passed the remainder of his saintly life almost as a religious recluse at Kingscliffe. In his earlier years he was conspicuous for his able controversial writings, both against Hoadly's Latitudinarian views on the Lord's Supper and also against the prominent Deistic writers, but in later life he became a celebrated advocate of Christian mysticism, and was greatly indebted to the writings of Jacob Behmen, the German pietist of the seventeenth century. "He could," he says, "hardly express the depth and fulness of Divine light and truth opened in Behmen's works by the grace and mercy of God." But although he inclined to take rather a narrow view of life, owing to his severely ascetic conduct, yet he was especially catholic in his sympathies, and loved truth from whatever quarter it might be advocated, and desired "to unite and join in heart and spirit with all that is Christian, holy, good and acceptable to God in all other Churches."[2]

It was, however, mainly owing to his masterpiece, the *Serious Call*, published in 1726, that Law exercised such a powerful influence on his own and succeeding generations. It was this work and its companion, *Christian Perfection*, which so powerfully moulded the earlier spiritual experiences of the Wesleys and many of the leading Evangelicals, while Dr. Johnson declared it was the first book that had made him in earnest about religion and described it as "the finest piece of hortatory theology in any language."[3]

Let us now consider briefly the growth and importance of Nonconformity during the century. It would appear that the cessation of religious persecution with the passing of the Toleration Act did not at first tend, as might have been expected, to a permanent increase in the numbers or spiritual activity of the Dissenters. As early as 1712 Daniel Defoe considered "the Dissenters' interest to be in a declining state," while by 1730 the "decay" of their cause had become a serious question amongst them. Mosheim wrote in 1741 that "those who are particularly acquainted with English affairs tell us that the Nonconformists

[1] Lathbury, *Hist. of Nonjurors*, ch. viii. p. 350 (1845).
[2] *Appeal to All that Doubt*, 2nd edn., 1756, p. 280.
[3] Boswell's *Life of Johnson*, i. 390.

diminish continually, and that this gradual diminution is ascribable to the mildness and gentleness of the bishops towards them."[1]

A vague and indefinite Latitudinarian theology, with its over-insistence on the rational obligation of moral duties rather than on distinctive Christian doctrines, was as conspicuous amongst Nonconformists as amongst Churchmen. Many of the old orthodox Presbyterian congregations were adopting Socinian or Unitarian opinions, and the same was in a large measure true of the General Baptists. In 1756 we are told that only two of the meeting-houses in the large towns of the North of England remained firm in their allegiance to the Trinitarian faith,[2] while Edmund Calamy, a prominent Dissenter, lamented in 1730 "that a real decay of serious religion, both in the Church and *out of it*, was very visible."[3] A recent eminent Nonconformist authority states also that "it must be admitted that a spirit of indifference respecting the masses of the people infected the respectable congregations gathered within the walls of Protestant meeting-houses."[4]

On the other hand, there were still a goodly number of Nonconformists who had not materially departed from the exemplary piety and strict orthodoxy of their Puritan forefathers. Thus the celebrated Dr. Isaac Watts, the author of the inspiring hymn, still so deservedly popular, "Our God, our help in ages past," faithfully ministered to an Independent congregation in Bury Street, St. Mary Axe, from 1702 to 1748; while Northampton from 1731 to 1750 was the scene of the equally devoted labours of another prominent hymn-writer, Philip Doddridge. The pious author of the once popular *Rise and Progress of Religion in the Soul*[5] combined the duties of pastor of the Independent Chapel and professor of the Dissenting Academy in that town.

There is no doubt that during the latter half of the century the Methodist Revival did much to stimulate the declining vitality of Nonconformity, especially among the independents, many new distinctly Evangelical congregations being formed; while the final alienation of the main body of Methodists from the Church was a very considerable numerical gain to the ranks of the

[1] *Eccles. Hist.* (Murdock's trans.), p. 872.
[2] *Cf.* Dale's *English Congregationalism*, p. 560 (1907).
[3] *Calamy's Life and Times*, ix. 531 (1829).
[4] Stoughton (*ante*), i. 292.
[5] This book is supposed to have been the means of the spiritual awakening of William Wilberforce.

Dissenters. This probably in a large measure accounted for the rapid growth of Nonconformity at this time, as a contemporary estimate at the end of the century gives their proportion to the Church as one to eight, whereas at the beginning it had been reckoned at one to twenty-two.

The relationship of Nonconformity to the Church during the greater part of the century was particularly harmonious; a sad want of spiritual zeal was characteristic of both, and the profession of a loose or unorthodox creed was a link which no doubt drew many nearer to one another. Strong personal friendship existed between many of the bishops and the leading Nonconformist divines. The famous Presbyterian, Samuel Chandler, maintained a close intimacy with his early schoolfellows Bishop Butler and Archbishop Secker, while Archbishop Herring and Bishop Warburton were on most friendly terms with Philip Doddridge. The majority of the Dissenters at this time were not hostile to the principle of a national establishment, and thus the time seemed specially propitious for renewing the attempts at "comprehension" which had been so often made in the latter part of the previous century. Although most of the Independents still adhered strongly to their cherished principles of Church government, yet the Presbyterians looked with favour on suggestions of union, while the Latitudinarian party in the Church regarded non-essential matters of discipline and ritual as quite immaterial "trifles," and strongly urged the historic comprehensiveness of the Anglican Communion, pleading that it had always included men of widely varying views, and was therefore well able to contain the extreme Puritan on the one hand and the high Anglican on the other. In 1748 some informal discussions on the subject took place between Samuel Chandler and Bishops Gooch and Sherlock, advocating a compromise on the basis of a more scriptural wording of the Articles, the elimination of the Athanasian Creed, and a conditional reordination of Dissenters. Archbishop Herring warmly supported the proposal, saying that "it was a very good thing and he wished it with all his heart"; but no practical result ensued, as in ecclesiastical matters the Government were still determined to act on Walpole's maxim and "not stir what was at rest." [1]

The amicable relations between Church and Dissent received a serious set-back at the time of the French Revolution, as many of the Nonconformists sympathised with the Republican cause,

[1] Doddridge's *Corres.*, v. 167.

while Churchmen were shocked at the inhuman excesses committed under the name of liberty. The cause of this changed feeling led to a somewhat singular reaction in favour of Romanists; because the sympathy felt by Churchmen for the exiled French priests, as sufferers on behalf of a common Christianity, rose superior to their old prejudice against them as adherents to the Romish faith. Bishop Horsley well voiced these sentiments when he said; "None, indeed, at this season are more entitled to our offices of love than those with whom the difference is wide in points of doctrine, discipline, and external rites—those venerable exiles, the prelates and clergy of the fallen Church of France, endeared to us by the edifying example they exhibit of patient suffering for conscience' sake."[1]

CHAPTER XIV

CHURCH LIFE OF THE CENTURY

LET us in conclusion glance briefly at the internal life and condition of the Church during this century, so conspicuous for its moral depravity and spiritual stagnation. It is not surprising that, in a cold and philosophical age of reason, with its intense dread of anything approaching "enthusiasm" in religion, but little interest should be taken in the æsthetic and symbolical side of public worship. Anything like elaborate or artistic design or ornamentation of sacred buildings was no product of the eighteenth century, while ritual or ornate ceremonialism in worship was entirely unknown. The scandal caused by Bishop Butler's representation of a cross on the east window of his chapel at Bristol is sufficient proof that there was no danger of Churches being ornamented with "popish" decorations.

Thus both the style of the material structures and the character of the services of the Church were of a specially dull, bare, and prosaic type. The fabrics, if not altogether neglected, were only just saved from decay, while so few new churches were erected that ecclesiastical architecture was becoming practically a lost art, a plentiful covering of whitewash too often defacing and concealing the artistic genius of a less unimaginative age. Even

[1] Horsley's *Sermons*, vol. iii. p. 320 (1816).

the cathedrals were often disfigured by some unlovely expressions of the popular Roman or Grecian style of architecture, while many of the parish churches were in a disgraceful condition of dirt and dilapidation. In the Carlisle diocese it was reported of one church that " the roof is so miserably shattered and broken that it cannot be safe sitting under it in stormy weather. Not one pane of glass in any of the windows. No flooring, no seats, no reading-desk. . . . There was no surplice to be found, nor did ever any such thing (as far as any present could remember) belong to this church." [1]

It was also during this century that pews became general in all churches, frequently high-backed and luxuriously furnished for the high-born and fashionable, carefully screening them from the vulgar gaze of the poor and less favoured, who, as a consequence of this invidious discrimination, were too often relegated to the dark and uncomfortable recesses of the building. It has been also asserted that in some cases wine and light refreshments were served between prayers and sermon to vary the monotony of a long service.[2]

The churchyards were in even a worse condition than the churches, being frequently used as pasture grounds for cattle, and the unoccupied portions for growing turnips or corn.

With the revival of Church life at the beginning of the century, the churches, especially in London and the large towns, had been well attended, and the services frequent. The daily office was performed twice in quite a number of churches, and Wednesday and Friday services were very general. The Saints' Days and great Festivals were also very carefully observed, but as the century advanced these evidences of religious zeal very largely disappeared. Daily services were almost unknown by the middle of our period, and even those on Wednesdays and Fridays were rare, while towards the end of the century there was very little observance of Saints' Days, or even of the great Festivals of the Church, with the general exception of Christmas Day. The congregations were often very irreverent in their behaviour, and were deplorably small in most places. One account states that " in the heart of the city of London on the Lord's day repeated instances have been known that not a single individual hath attended divine service." [3] Wesley, in justifying his practice

[1] *Miscellany Accounts of Diocese of Carlisle*, p. 54 (1877).
[2] Cf. *Eng. Ch. in 18th Cent.*, p. 412.
[3] T. Haweis, *Church of England Vindicated*, p. 40 (1801).

of field preaching, stated: "I wonder at those who talk of the *indecency* of field preaching. The highest *indecency* is in St. Paul's church, where a considerable part of the congregation are asleep, or talking, or looking about, not minding a word the preacher says." [1]

Frequently the performance of morning prayer alone was considered sufficient on Sundays, while the prevalent custom of non-residence, where several adjacent parishes were served by one curate, must have often rendered more than this impossible. In Essex, in 1763, we are told "that only 102 of the 310 churches were even supposed to have two services a Sunday, and some had only one service a fortnight, and some only one a month." [2]

The Sacraments were fearfully neglected, and except in the cathedrals the Lord's Supper was seldom administered more than four times a year. Bishop Secker in his second Charge, in 1741, urges that "one thing might be done in all your parishes . . . a Sacrament might easily be interposed in that long interval between Whitsuntide and Christmas . . . and if afterwards you can advance from a quarterly Communion to a monthly I make no doubt you will," [3] while as late as Easter Day 1800, only six people communicated at St. Paul's Cathedral.

The prejudice, so largely entertained in the latter part of the previous century, against bringing children to the church for baptism, had not been entirely overcome, a strong preference still often existing for private baptisms.

We have already noticed the decline in the character of preaching, and as the century advanced the pulpit lost more and more of the spiritual power and influence it had exercised at the time of the Reformation and under the Puritan régime, and it was not until the closing years of our period that the results of the earnest evangelistic appeals of the Methodist revivalists once again demonstrated the importance of the ministry of the Word. Cowper, in trying to describe the true apostolic preacher, asks if the picture in any way resembles

> "The things that mount the rostrum with a skip,
> And then skip down again; pronounce a text,
> Cry hem! and reading what they never wrote,
> Just fifteen minutes, huddle up their work,
> And with a well-bred whisper close the scene." [4]

[1] Southey, p. 217.
[2] *Cf.* Balleine (*ante*), p. 19.
[3] *Secker's Charges*, pp. 62–3.
[4] *Poetical Works*, p. 245, "The Task."

It would seem that the contempt entertained for the clergy as a class, which had been so conspicuous a feature of the Restoration period, was still maintained. A modern authority affirms that "there never had been a time when the established ministers of religion were held in so much contempt as in the Hanoverian period, or when satire upon Churchmen was so congenial to the general feeling," although he is careful to point out that "there was no feeling against the Church establishment . . . the contempt was for the persons, manners, and character of the ecclesiastics . . . The unedifying lives of the clergy are a standard theme of sarcasm and continue to be so till a late period in the century." [1]

A contemporary statement in the reign of George II., however, affirms that "the clergy were generally pious and exemplary." [2] But although the bishops and clergy themselves cannot be charged with leading immoral lives, yet it is feared they were too often careless and culpable in their personal conduct, or at least did little to counteract immorality in others. In spite of Lord (Chancellor) Thurlow's living openly with a mistress, "his house," we are told, "was not only frequented by his brother the bishop, but by ecclesiastics of all degrees, who celebrated the orthodoxy of the head of the law and his love of the Established Church." [3]

Archbishop Cornwallis openly displayed his worldliness by holding routs at Lambeth Palace on Sundays as well as weekdays. After twice vainly endeavouring, by personal interviews, to convince the primate of the evil influence of such inconsistent conduct, Lady Huntingdon sought the intervention of the King. George III., whose personal life and influence were of so entirely opposite a character, wrote a severe letter to the Archbishop, reprimanding him strongly for encouraging so much unseemly dissipation in "a place where so many of your predecessors have led their lives in such sanctity as has thrown lustre on the pure religion they professed and adorned. I trust you will suppress them immediately, so that I may not have occasion to show any further marks of my displeasure or to interpose in a different manner." [4]

[1] *Essays and Reviews*, pp. 315, 316.
[2] Smollett's *Continuation of Hume*, v. 375 (1791).
[3] Campbell's *Lives of the Chancellors*, viii. 314.
[4] *Countess of Huntingdon and her Circle*, p. 125.

We can only hope that Cowper slightly overcolours his account of the generality of the clergy of the period when he describes them as: —

> "Loose in morals, and in manners vain,
> In conversation frivolous, in dress
> Extreme, at once rapacious and profuse,
> Frequent in park with lady at his side,
> Ambling and prattling scandal as he goes,
> But rare at home, and never at his books;
> Constant at routs, familiar with a round
> Of ladyships, a stranger to the poor;
> Ambitious of preferment for its gold,
> And well prepared by ignorance and sloth,
> By infidelity and love of the world,
> To make God's work a sinecure; a slave
> To his own pleasures and his patron's pride." [1]

Undoubtedly the most serious and harmful fault of the clergy was their adoption of the worldly self-seeking aims so common to their age. The solemn and sacred responsibilities to their flocks were too often entirely ignored in their insatiable desire to enhance their social position and their temporal prosperity. "Preferment"-hunting seemed to be the main object of those who were set apart to "feed and provide for the Lord's family and seek for Christ's sheep that are dispersed abroad." [2] As we have already noticed, pluralities and non-residence were shockingly common, and what was conspicuous of the bishops and dignitaries applied equally to the inferior clergy. Bishop Herring held the deanery of Rochester with the bishopric of Bangor, while the deanery of Westminster was usually held in conjunction with the bishopric of Rochester. We can scarcely wonder at non-resident incumbents when Bishop Hoadly held the see of Bangor for six years without, apparently, ever visiting his diocese! So usual had the practice become during the century, that in 1785 Paley recommends the non-resident clergy to content themselves with distributing S.P.C.K. tracts to their neglected parishioners, while Bishop Horsley as late as 1796, in his Charge actually condones the abuse by asserting that "many non-residents are promoting the general cause of Christianity, and perhaps doing better service than if they confined themselves to the ordinary labours of the ministry."

[1] *Poetical Works*, p. 245. [2] *Ordering of Priests*.

Another grave abuse which existed throughout this century was the glaring inequality of the material and social condition of the dignitaries and inferior clergy. Bentley asserted that six thousand of the clergy had not more than an average income of £50 a year. [1] This may in some cases explain and excuse the "pluralism" so common with many beneficed clergy. The position of the unbeneficed clergy was scandalous. There could be little affinity between the bishop who lived sumptuously in his palace or rode in state through the country, preceded by his lackeys, and the humble, hard-worked curate on £40, or at the most £50 a year; as till 1796 it was illegal to fix the stipends of unbeneficed clergy beyond this amount. A contemporary clergyman who wrote a book to describe *The Myseries and Great Hardships of the Inferior Clergy* states that the curates' "salaries were often less than the sextons', and not so punctually paid; that the rectors made jests upon their poverty, and that the common fee for a sermon was a shilling and a dinner, and for reading the prayers twopence and a cup of coffee." [2]

We must not, however, forget that the religious spirit of the nation and the spiritual activity of the Church were deepened and quickened in no small measure owing to the work and influence of the Methodist revival. Earnest and devout congregations flocked in large numbers to the Evangelical churches, which were multiplying fast towards the end of the century. Week-night services, Sunday-schools, and classes for Bible instruction were being started in many parishes by the zealous Evangelical clergy, whose work, it has been asserted, "unquestionably effected a great moral revolution in England." "They gradually changed the whole spirit of the English Church. They infused into it a new fire and passion of devotion, kindled a spirit of fervent philanthropy, raised the standard of clerical duty, and completely altered the whole tone and tendency of the preaching of its ministers." [3] By the end of the century the general sneer at and abuse of religious "enthusiasts" had almost died down, or were being more properly transferred to the idle "pluralist" who neglected his cure.

But although the Evangelical party were undoubtedly the most active force in the Church at this time, and had done so much to restore vital religion in the country, so that Mr. Lecky

[1] *Essays and Reviews*, p. 309.
[2] Quoted in Overton and Relton, p. 273.
[3] Lecky, *Hist. of Eng. in 18th Cent.*, ii. pp. 600 and 627.

affirms that "before the close of the century the Evangelical movement had become dominant in England, and continued the almost undisputed centre of religion till the rise of the Tractarian movement in 1830,"[1] yet it would be wrong to suppose that they ever formed the majority either of the clergy or laity. The Evangelicals were powerful as a spiritual rather than as a numerical force, and thus the spiritual torpor and apathy, still so largely prevalent, was not fully grappled with until a generation or so later. For, despite its extravagant tendencies and dangerous development, it was the Oxford Movement, although conducted on widely different and to a large extent contradictory lines, which yet supplemented the efforts of the Evangelicals in once more generally restoring a zealous and active, if not always sound and healthy, Church life.

[1] Ibid., ii. p. 627.

INDEX

Printed in Great Britain by
Butler & Tanner Ltd.,
Frome and London